SOFTWARE TEAMING

*A Mob Programming,
Whole-Team Approach*

Woody Zuill
and
Kevin Meadows

Second Edition

Software Teaming – A Mob Programming, Whole-Team Approach

Copyright © 2022 by Woody Zuill and Kevin Meadows

All Rights Reserved.

Cover designed by Woody Zuill and Kevin Meadows

Printed in the United States of America

First Printing: November 2022

ISBN-9798361186938

Woody Zuill

Dedicated to Eugene Zuill – my Dad. A brilliant engineer, businessman, and kind human being. From him, I learned a great deal about collaboration, teamwork, selflessness, and "kindness, consideration, and respect."

Kevin Meadows

Dedicated to Gene and Nadine for showing the virtue of persistence and the power of asking "why?" Oh, and never forget, "Voca cum adveneris."

"It would be better if everyone worked together as a system, with the aim for everybody to win."

W. EDWARDS DEMING

Contents

Acknowledgments

Woody's

Llewellyn Falco - for way too many things: Driver-Navigator, my first introduction to Coding Dojos, noticing our team was "working together all day long" and telling other people about it, endless and continuous encouragement, collaboration on presentations, coding, thinking... and so much more.

My wife, Andrea Zuill, for all the art and illustrations - I love her, and I love her art. Nice combination!!! And for always being ready to help me think things through.

The original Hunter Crew: Dan Yeung Wong, Gordon Pu, Dexter Baga, and Chris Lucian. Also: Marc Kase (my manager), Aaron Griffith (our first addition to the Mob), Jason Kerney (our second addition to the Mob), and all the folks at Hunter Industries.

Amazing Agile folks: Linda Rising, Rachael Davies, Diana Larsen, Esther Derby, Ainsley Nies, Nancy Van Schooenderwoert, Elisabeth Hendrickson, Rebecca Wirfs-Brock, June Clarke, Johanna Rothman, Chris Chapman, Joe Yoder, and many others.

The Swedish Contingent: Ville Svärd, Tobias Anderberg, Marcus Hammarberg, Lennart Fridén, Gianfranco Alongi, Eric Schon, Håkan Forss, Agical, Aptitud, Tretton 37, Ericsson, and Øredev...and many others.

Chris Lucian at Hunter Industries for his help with the Remote Software Teaming chapter.

The original San Diego Visual Basic Users Group, where Kevin and Woody met.

Kevin's

All the folks I worked with over the years who helped me along my software journey. There are too many to list, but that doesn't mean I don't appreciate each and every one of you.

Woody's original Software Teaming group, who welcomed me to watch and learn what they were doing when it was still a new idea. Plus, they bought me lunch and gave me a hat. How can you beat that?

The great people at the original San Diego Visual Basic User Group, who freely gave (and probably still give!) so much helpful advice and pointed out the path ahead.

Chris Lucian for his excellent feedback on Remote Software Teaming.

The "Cohorts Group," for their excellent ideas about being more Agile: Chris, Alfredo, David, Woody, and Fred. Thanks, guys.

Foreword

By Kent Beck

How good can we be at software development?

I grew up in a 60s and 70s Silicon Valley full of possibility and optimism. My dad was a geek. His friends were geeks. Enormous changes were coming & they all knew geeks would be at the heart.

When it was my turn to push the geek agenda forward I didn't hold back. That's why I called it "Extreme" programming. Everything good about development cranked up to 11.

How naïve. What I thought was 11 was really more like a 6. Continuous integration became continuous deployment. Month-long iterations became week-long iterations. And now pairing becomes teaming.

I admire Woody & Kevin for their principles/experience/judgement process. If you want to make progress you can't start with judgement. You'll never change the frame by judging within the frame. Instead, they started with the principles of maximizing collaboration & learning, experimented with how to best achieve those goals, & then judged the result.

Here's the beauty of Mob Programming--it's a nearly-zero-risk experiment. If you don't like it, don't do it. If you don't think you'd like it, then you'll never really know. Which might be okay. But if you want to know just how good we can be at software development, it's worth an experiment.

Part One: Introduction

Illustration © 2013 - Andrea Zuill

This part of the book introduces Software Teaming and gives an overview of its approach. We explain the basics, show you what it looks like, and explain how it started. When you finish this section, you should understand the big picture of Software Teaming.

1   What is Software Teaming?

Illustration © 2015 · Andrea Zuill

Software Teaming is a software development approach where the whole team works together on the same thing, at the same time, in the same space, and at the same computer. This is similar to Pair Programming, where two people sit at the same computer and collaborate on the same code at the same time. However, with Software Teaming, we extend the collaboration to everyone on the team while still using a single computer for writing the code and doing other work.

In addition to software coding, the team works together to do almost all the work a typical software development team tackles, such as defining stories, designing, testing, and deploying software. Nearly all work is handled as "working meetings" or workshops, and all the people involved in creating the software are considered team members, including the customer/product owner. Many teams work this way, more or less all day long, every day.

In other words, this is an evolutionary step beyond the Extreme Programming concept of Pair Programming. We strive to accentuate and amplify concepts such as face-to-face and side-by-side communication, team alignment, collaboration, whole team involvement, continuous code review, and the "self-organizing team."

How We Started

We didn't seek to invent a new way to work or extend the idea of Pair Programming. We simply noticed some things working well for us and expanded on them. We regularly held practice sessions using a Coding Dojo approach where everyone uses a single computer with a projector and passes the keyboard around.

At one point, we needed to restart work on a product that had been on hold for several months. We gathered to look at it and decide how to take on the job. Rather than simply investigating, we immediately started refactoring the code, and it was natural for us to pass the keyboard around as we did. We held a retrospective at the end of the day, and we all felt the experience was very positive. We decided to continue working together, in the same way, the next day. We haven't stopped since and have successfully delivered many products and enhancements over the years since we started Software Teaming.

What's in a Name?

Software Teaming is our more recent name for describing how we work together as a group, with the whole team working together on the same thing, at the same time, in the same space, and at the same computer. Many people probably know its more popular term, "Mob Programming," a phrase initially coined in the early days.

We've adopted the new name for two reasons. First, some people are perhaps unsure about something that includes the word "Mob." Second, we believe that "Teaming" is a word that captures how complex problems must be solved today: as teams instead of as individuals. We derive our new phrase from Amy Edmondson's excellent book "Teaming" [1], which we highly recommend.

A story from Woody: People often ask how Mob Programming got its name.

While I now prefer to use the term "Software Teaming," I originally called it "Whole Team Programming" for my first-ever talk at the Open Jam at Agile 2012 in Dallas, TX. However, I was already using the term "Mob Programming" for the Coding Dojos I facilitated at user groups and code camps. As a joke, I would say, "this is like Pair Programming, but with more people, sort of a mob, but we don't want it to be chaotic, so we have some simple guidelines." I first heard the term Mob Programming used in a paper from an early XP conference. It was published in the book "*Extreme Programming Perspectives*" in 2002.

In Coding Dojos I held at user groups and conferences before we worked this way, I used many of these techniques that we now use in Software Teaming. So while I preferred "Whole Team Programming," people started asking about Mob Programming, and I wasn't going to try to go against the tide, so to speak.

I have no preference. I called it Whole Team Programming, and while I quickly changed to calling it Mob Programming, I have always said I don't care what it's called. Learning to work well as a team is worthwhile, and I invite people to call it what they will.

I've heard others use "Ensemble Programming" (although that term is ambiguous) and a few other things. But as I said, I don't care what we call it as long as people have a chance to learn about it and try it.

To be clear, Software Teaming is merely a tiny evolutionary step beyond Pair Programming. There are no rules except the general guideline of, "Let's figure out how to turn up our ability to collaborate well."

People can call it whatever works best for their situation.

Why this Book?

In a way, Software Teaming is the story of how one team discovered how they wanted to work. We shared our "new" workstyle as people heard about it. We invited them to visit us to see for themselves, and we got invited to share at user group meetings and Agile conferences. This book is a result of that sharing.

Software Teaming grew out of a few simple ideas:

- The people doing the work can best figure out how to do that work.
- We can get a lot of benefits out of studying and practicing together.
- Getting good results from retrospectives is essential.
- Pay attention to what's working, and look for ways to Turn Up the Good.

Software Teaming is an outgrowth of paying attention to providing an environment where everyone can excel in their work. We hope your team can benefit from understanding and applying the idea of creating and protecting such an environment, and perhaps something like Software Teaming will happen for you.

In other words, Software Teaming isn't necessarily universally applicable, but the idea of working well together might be. Follow along on our journey as we share our ideas about what we've done and learned.

References

1. Edmondson, Amy. Teaming. Wiley India, 2012.

2   Set the Stage for Great Things

Illustration © 2012 · Andrea Zuill

Create and Maintain an Environment Where Great Things Can Happen

Here's a wonderful quote from Robert Henri:

"The object isn't to make art. It's to be in that wonderful state which makes art inevitable."

Robert Henri

Software Teaming "happened" because we follow a fundamental philosophy: having an environment where awesome things can happen almost guarantees that awesome things WILL happen. We've had enough experience with this to feel confident it's worth paying attention to this idea.

> *An environment where awesome things can happen almost guarantees that awesome things WILL happen.*

The Agile Manifesto and Principles (see Appendices) give excellent guidance on things to heed. Here are some ideas we used to create an environment where great things could happen.

Self-organizing teams: the people doing the work can best determine how to do that work.

Communicating face-to-face and customer collaboration: business people and developers work together daily, so it's easy for everyone to work with each other side-by-side.

Individuals over process: treat people with Kindness, Consideration, and Respect, and great things happen.

Trust them to get the job done: make the work environment safe. Having this safety makes it more likely that people will express ideas that turn out to be great.

Reflect, Tune, and Adjust: practice continuous improvement. Study and Practice together.

Turn up the Good: as Extreme Programming's Kent Beck stated, "I had the mental image of knobs on a control board. Each knob was a practice that, from experience, I knew worked well. I would turn all the knobs up to ten and see what happened."

These ideas might look different for every company, but the fundamental concept is the same. When we use the Agile Manifesto values and principles as guidelines for evaluating a practice or technique, we set the stage for greatness.

We Work Better When We Work Together

As you can see, working together is a basic tenet of Agile software development. The Agile Manifesto Values and Principles state this or, at least, hint at this concept: let's work together on the same thing, at the same time, and in the same space. Much of what humans have accomplished has happened because people have worked together.

Software Teaming nudges the Agile idea of working together a bit further by introducing the notion that designing, writing code, testing, and other tasks can be done with a group of people at the same computer.

Software Teaming

All the brilliant minds working together

on the same thing…
at the same time…
in the same space…
at the same computer

The Stage was Set

Software Teaming is the story of how one team self-organized. Something wonderful emerged by setting the stage for collaboration, sustainability, and other Agile Principles. It's doubtful this would have occurred if we weren't working in an environment where great things could happen.

3   A View of the Room

From the Front

A few things to notice:

- Only one computer is being used for coding.
- There are other computers used for other things.
- There are two keyboards, but there could be more or less.
- There are two mice.
- Only one keyboard and mouse are in use at any one time.
- Everyone finds a spot they like and where they can see well.

From the Back

A few other things to notice:

- We each have our own personalized chair.
- We're a comfortable distance apart from each other.
- We can easily turn to each other and talk.
- There are whiteboards and flip charts.
- We have flip chart pages from our retrospectives in view.
- Our team agreement is always visible.

4 See for Yourself

Watch a Video of a Full Day of Work in Only Three Minutes

It can be challenging to imagine what Software Teaming looks like without actually experiencing it. The next best thing might be a video.

You can see the video at this link or by searching for it:

https://bit.ly/3OdjXzt

The video shows our team working an eight-hour day. We've condensed it into three minutes to show what it's like to work together all day. You'll notice a lot of talking, moving, sharing, laughing, thinking, coding, testing, and taking breaks as needed.

You can see that we have made it comfortable for everyone. Each person chooses the keyboard they want to use and has their own personalized chair. We sit far enough apart for comfort but close enough to communicate easily across the team. Everyone has their own private work area if they want to work alone.

At the time of this video, our product owners or business experts would visit us for an hour or two each day. They would review what we just completed and help us place it into Production. They would then decide on the next work item and work with us to understand it.

We come in at about the same time each morning, take lunch at about the same time and end the day at the same time. Otherwise, it would be hard to work as a team.

5 How We Discovered Software Teaming

Illustration © 2012 · Andrea Zuill

How did Software Teaming come into being? Was it the result of a research laboratory? Was it invented by a mad genius working in the dead of night? Was it created by an expert team of process control gurus? Actually, it was a gradual, evolutionary process best described as a "try it and see" approach. Indeed, it was simply a series of logical next steps in how Agile work was already being done. As you'll see, we discovered these steps one by one and serendipitously found our way to Software Teaming.

The Driver-Navigator Model

Around 2007, I (Woody) was doing basic Pair Programming with a local Agilist named Llewellyn Falco. Instead of the typical approach of each programmer taking turns with the keyboard to code while explaining their thought process, Llewellyn suggested using something called the Driver-Navigator model.

In this approach, the programmers still take turns, but one is the Driver doing all the typing while the other is the Navigator explaining the idea to translate into code. The Navigator is responsible for thinking through the logic and purpose of the idea. The Driver is responsible for translating that into code. Llewellyn's crucial point was that for an idea to go from someone's head into the computer, it must go through someone else's hands.

We would switch roles whenever the Driver had an idea to contribute. For example, we would switch roles if I were driving and felt I had a good idea for the next step. I would become the Navigator, and Llewellyn would become the Driver at the keyboard.

Once I learned and began using Llewellyn's model, I realized how much more effective this was for me and decided to continue using it in my work.

The Coding Dojo Sessions

A few years later, Llewellyn and I were facilitating a Coding Dojo session at a code camp. The idea was to have groups of four or five people working at a computer trying to solve a given exercise. They would compare results and discuss what they learned when everyone was done.

We did something different in this instance by using a timer. Every few minutes, the person at the keyboard would switch out with someone else in their group. It was probably the first time we had applied the Driver-Navigator model to more than just a pair. It seemed to flow well, and everyone enjoyed working in this model. We decided to try this approach at future code camps, user groups, and conferences and found the results equally satisfying.

Studying and Practicing Together

A year or two later, I was at a new job helping the team explore an Agile approach. We set aside three hours every Friday to study and practice together to become better programmers. It was always voluntary. We diligently held our sessions every week, but no one was forced to participate.

Our study topics included Test-Driven Development, refactoring, language features, and problem-solving skills. Leveraging my code conference experiences with the Coding Dojos, we decided to do our code exercises using the Driver-Navigator model with the whole team while rotating the Driver every four minutes. We really liked it. We learned a lot from each other and became a better-functioning programming team. Some team members started regularly pairing in their daily work, and all of us were noticeably improving.

The Next (In)Obvious Steps

It wasn't long before we faced problems with a complex product that needed urgent attention. This product was complicated and had shortcomings in the design and code. Some developers were already working on it and realized they wanted help from the rest of the team to get the product into shape.

We grabbed a conference room so all of us could look at the product's current state and try to get a shared understanding of the problems we faced. Our main goal was to figure out how we would tackle this work. For example, "Who would do what? What should we do first? What were the most critical problems?"

Everyone pitched in, and we reviewed the product's documents and code. As we started this work, we naturally began following the Driver-Navigator model we had used in our Coding Dojos. Someone noticed an improvement we could make to some method names, handed the keyboard to someone else, and began to navigate the needed change.

We continued working this way until someone needed the conference room, and we had to leave. At that point, our scheduled meeting time was over.

We could have felt blocked and simply returned to our cubicles, abandoning our teamwork. Instead, one of the team members said, "Let's go find an empty conference room so we can keep working on this," and everyone agreed. We noticed something good happening. We had just enjoyed a few fruitful hours of wonderful teamwork and wanted it to continue.

We moved to the available room. Upon arriving, a team member suggested we should book another room to use when time ran out for this room. Again, we noticed something good was happening and wanted to "Turn it up."

The rest of that day, we worked as a team, following the Driver-Navigator model and working on the code. At the day's end, we held a short retrospective to discuss how things went. We decided we liked working as a team and wanted to continue it the next day. We found a conference room for the following day and continued our team approach.

We followed this basic pattern of working together, moving from room to room over the next few weeks. We reviewed how the day went each day and decided to keep working "as a team." We felt our approach rapidly improved our communication ability, increased our knowledge, and helped us find better solutions. We were gaining a deep and shared understanding of the product and the technologies involved.

About this time, we decided to call what we were doing "Mob Programming," which eventually became "Software Teaming."

We found a small workroom we could use on a semi-permanent basis and set it up with a projector and team desk. Eventually, we rearranged our cubicle workstations to accommodate this style of work. Fast forward several years, and we were still Software Teaming, never looking back.

In hindsight, it seems like an obvious way of working that simply required connecting the clearly-defined dots. In foresight, it was anything but. One thing helping us along the path was that we already had experience working together as a team during our weekly Dojo sessions. In fact, it's unlikely that we would have taken to Software Teaming if we had only worked individually. It wasn't a "huge leap" but rather many baby steps moving from "individuals" to "team." Our attitude of "try it and see," or better yet, "inspect and adapt," allowed us to be open to experimentation. This experimentation led us step by step into new directions and gradually down the path of discovering Software Teaming as a way of working.

6   Quick Start Guide

Let's start with something essential: keep it simple and take baby steps. There's no "one right way." Being flexible is vital because nothing we tell you is written in stone. These are just ideas for a starting place. There's no "one size fits all" set of rules. We think it works better if you pay attention, notice what's working, and adapt as needed.

Here are some ideas that have worked well for getting started:

- Size of team: four or five people.
- Attendance and participation are voluntary.
- Arrange a physical setup that's comfortable and simple to put together and use.
- Follow the Driver-Navigator model.
- Use a rotation time of four or five minutes.
- Work on an exercise.
- Do it weekly: for two to three hours, or daily for one to two hours.
- Invite anyone interested.
- Try to show Kindness, Consideration, and Respect.
- Hold a short retrospective after each session.

We cover each of these in more detail below.

Size of Team: Four or Five People

It's easier to start small and scale up as you gain experience. A frequent turn at the keyboard is comforting to those used to spending all day there. Also, we need to get used to quickly taking the keyboard and releasing it. With four or five members, everyone gets more practice doing this.

If you have more than this number, consider creating another team and experimenting with approaches to see what works best.

Attendance and Participation are Voluntary

The critical point is that no one is forced to join. Everyone is invited and can participate if they choose. They're also free to stop participating if they choose.

A Physical Setup that's Comfortable, Simple to Assemble, and Use

It's great if you have a permanent workspace for Software Teaming. At first, however, it might be necessary to use a temporary space. We've seen a variety of setups, and they all seem to work well. Collaboration can be done virtually if your team works remotely by using video conferencing and screen-sharing tools.

A standard conference room is the first choice for many teams, typically with a long table and a screen at one end. This approach isn't the best because it's difficult to switch Drivers, and the seating is suboptimal for comfort. It often results in back, neck, and eye strain.

If you must use a conference room and have the freedom to change things, have everyone sit on the long side of the table with a large screen in front of them.

Any available monitor or projector is probably workable with some thought. Usually, it's best to have a large enough monitor for everyone to see easily, but you can use several smaller monitors. Try to be flexible.

Our Preferred Setup

We have found this setup to work very well and have seen it at many companies. You can have one, two, or more monitors. Experiment with monitor height to ensure its position works well for everyone.

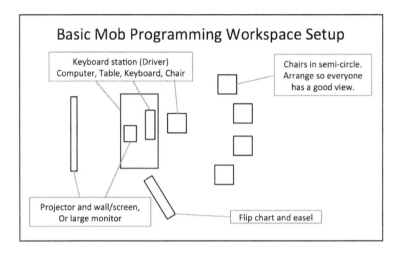

A Laptop and Larger Monitor on a Table

This arrangement is easy to set up and remove whenever you want to put together a Software Teaming station quickly. It also works well for a permanent setup.

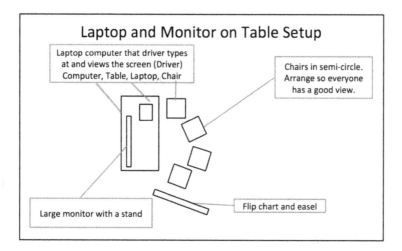

The "Triangle" Setup

This setup uses three monitors with three keyboards. It's good if there's limited space. One or two people can sit at each monitor/keyboard station. This arrangement works well when you don't have a large monitor. As with the other setups, there's one computer, and the monitors mirror the same display.

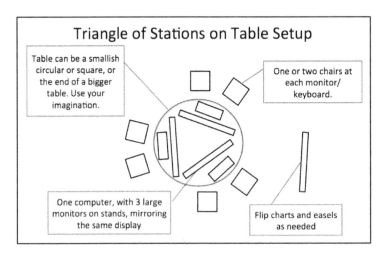

Triangle of Stations on Table Setup

Table can be a smallish circular or square, or the end of a bigger table. Use your imagination.

One or two chairs at each monitor/keyboard.

One computer, with 3 large monitors on stands, mirroring the same display

Flip charts and easels as needed

Follow the Driver–Navigator Model

The Driver–Navigator model is our preferred approach for Software Teaming. A brief introduction follows. More detail is in the chapter The Driver–Navigator Model in Depth.

The basic arrangement is that one member of the Software Teaming group is the Driver doing the typing. In contrast, the others are the Navigators thinking, discussing, diagramming, and sharing ideas that will become code. The Navigators are responsible for thinking through the ideas' logic and purpose, and the Driver is responsible for translating that into code.

"For an idea to go from someone's head into the computer, it must go through someone else's hands."

Llewellyn Falco

Requiring an idea to go through someone else's hands leads to a better understanding of ideas that become code. After an agreed-upon time, the roles switch, and someone else becomes the Driver. With practice, the rotation becomes easy and natural. For us, we use the timer to establish a rotation interval, but you can choose a way of rotating that works best for your team.

Regardless of your rotation approach, it's worthwhile to practice the following things:

- Allow others to speak.
- Seek their ideas.
- Ask questions as needed.
- Pause occasionally during the work to have discussions without coding.

This style of working doesn't always come naturally. It takes deliberate effort to allow everyone, especially the quiet voices, to have their say.

Use a Rotation Time of Four or Five Minutes

We cover the rotation specifics in The Driver-Navigator Model in Depth, but we suggest rotating the Driver every four to five minutes when you first begin Software Teaming. This interval allows everyone a frequent turn as the Driver. It also keeps the Driver's turn short, preventing the Driver from working without direction from the Navigators. Once you gain experience, you can always experiment with different intervals. Remember: not everyone needs to take the keyboard.

Work on an Exercise

We suggest starting Software Teaming with safe code so you can experiment in a sandbox without concern for something going wrong. The Software Teaming group will likely be more relaxed, have more fun, and be more open to learning if they aren't under the additional pressure of working on Production code. Simple exercises like coding a game of Tic-Tac-Toe can be a great place to start.

Where can you find simple exercises to work on? One great source is Emily Bache's excellent book, "*The Coding Dojo Handbook*" [1]. She provides a catalog of interesting and simple exercises called Code Katas. A Code Kata is a small, fun problem that shouldn't take more than an hour or two to solve.

We believe that Code Katas are more than just puzzles to solve. They are a powerful way of learning coding concepts and techniques. They make excellent, simple exercises for learning Software Teaming with your team.

You can also find Code Katas online. A quick internet search will yield many sites with engaging, fun exercises.

You can do the same exercises more than once. You can try them with different Software Teaming setups so the team can experiment and determine which setup produces the best result.

Once the Software Teaming group gains experience and is fluent with the basics, they can graduate to live code.

Do it Weekly for Two to Three Hours or Daily for One to Two Hours

The idea is to start small and scale up as you gain experience. As with anything new, it generally flows more smoothly when introduced gradually. This approach gives the team time to reflect and make desired adjustments. There's no strict rule, but a few hours per day or week should be sufficient to understand the Software Teaming process.

Of course, the team may find they're making rapid progress and wish to scale up to more hours. That's their prerogative, and they shouldn't be required to scale up unless they're ready.

Invite Anyone Interested

Perhaps only your programmers will be interested at first. However, you might consider including a cross-section of team members, such as coders, testers, product experts, managers, and coaches. A broader cross-section can be a bonus because you get diverse perspectives. Software Teaming has worked well for us by taking advantage of this collective intelligence.

Strive to make it comfortable for those who can't code or are unwilling to take the keyboard. Taking the keyboard should be optional. Software Teaming is about quickly sharing ideas, discussing them, and proving them. Work to keep everyone involved as active participants in the discussions and idea generation. Not everyone has to write code.

Try to Show Kindness, Consideration, and Respect

An essential practice of Software Teaming is treating each other with Kindness, Consideration, and Respect. We cover this in detail in Kindness, Consideration, and Respect, but for now, let's state its importance to Software Teaming's success.

Why is this so important? Working as a team means we spend much more time interacting than usual. Treating each other with Kindness, Consideration, and Respect means we can avoid the resentments, anger, and unhappiness that can often burden a team. It isn't always easy, and it isn't always instinctive, but things will flow much more smoothly if you try your best.

Hold a Short Retrospective After Each Session

After each session, take time to do a short retrospective. It's helpful to ask questions like, "Should we do more of what went well? Should we change what didn't go well?" Retrospectives help the team reflect, tune their approach, and adjust for the next session. They also help you discover a Software Teaming style that works best for your team. Using this kind of iterative, evolutionary approach will help the team be more successful.

References

1.   Bache, Emily. The Coding Dojo Handbook. LeanPub, 2103.

Part Two: The Details

Illustration © 2013 - Andrea Zuill

This part of the book dives into the details of Software Teaming. We describe how a typical Software Teaming group is structured, its work environment, the details of the Driver-Navigator model, and address questions regarding why we want to work this way. When you finish this section, you should understand enough to attempt Software Teaming in your work environment.

1   The Software Teaming Group

Illustration © 2015 - Andrea Zuill

Who belongs to the Software Teaming group? It's a simple question, but the answer isn't so simple.

Who Belongs On the Team?

The vague answer is "It Depends." Ideally, everyone who can provide useful input on a product is a candidate. When these people are brought together, many wonderful things quickly happen. Decisions get made, exercised, validated, modified, abandoned, or proved by actual use in Production, and we rapidly steer to the next interesting thing. It's the heightened and immediate interactions that we want.

It might not always be possible to gather all these people on a single team and have them work together all day, every day. However, some subset of "all the people" can be good enough. Those doing the work can figure out the right mix for any situation.

We don't feel it's appropriate to make a blanket recommendation regarding who belongs on the team. We'll share what we've done, but each team should decide for themselves.

Here are the guidelines we use:

- If we frequently find we're blocked because we're missing knowledge, we probably need to add a team member.

- We also borrow from Open Space technology: if you feel you're adding value or learning, welcome to the team! If you think you aren't adding value or learning, find a place where you feel you can.

Our Story

In our original Software Teaming group, we had four programmers, one tester, and a facilitator who worked together all day, every day. Our team composition changed over time. Our product experts couldn't spend "all day, every day" with the team. In the best cases, they would join us daily for an hour or two and make themselves available for quick meetings and phone calls whenever we needed their input. There were several other "occasional" team members. Most frequently, this would be our database administrator, but there were others.

When we worked with people in other departments, they would join us whenever they could. Part-time members aren't as beneficial as working together all the time because we lose shared team memory, rapid decision-making, and quick feedback. Part-time members also require frequent context switching. However, the "core team" of the developers, testers, and facilitators helped us retain some of these benefits. We filled in the gaps with large, visible information boards, frequent demonstrations of the work in progress, and daily delivery into Production.

We've had sessions with up to fourteen people when the work was urgent, and the knowledge was scattered throughout the company. We all worked together on the same thing, at the same time, in the same space, and at a single computer. This large group was effective. We made rapid progress by having the knowledge and participation of every individual.

So, start with what you have or can get, experiment, modify as needed, and find ways to fill in the gaps. Pay attention and always Turn Up the Good as best you can, given your situation.

2   The Workspace Setup

Illustration © 2014 - Andrea Zuill

The workspace setup is vital for a comfortable Software Teaming environment. There's a lot to consider, such as ease of use and comfort.

The Area

Most of our work is performed while sitting together in the group work area. We try to make it as comfortable as possible. There's plenty of room, and we can easily have others join us when needed.

Our work area is configured from standard cubicle walls and is about sixteen feet by eighteen feet. This area is part of a larger group of cubicles, so we must mind our volume to avoid bothering others nearby, but this setup works nicely.

We find that a standard conference room with a long table and a screen at one end is the first choice for many teams because of its ease of setup. It isn't desirable long-term because it's difficult to switch Drivers, and the seating is sub-optimal for comfort. It often results in back, neck, and eye strain. Instead, here are some better setups from various teams around the world.

Our Preferred Setup

We find this setup to work very well and have seen it at many companies. You can have one, two, or more monitors. Experiment with monitor height so it works well for everyone. The larger the monitors or projection, the better. The working area has plenty of room for everyone.

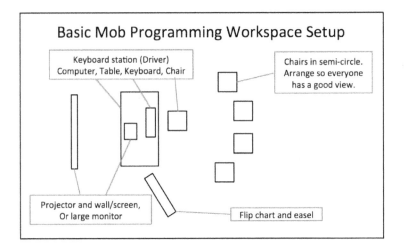

A Laptop and Larger Monitor on a Table

This arrangement is easy to set up and remove whenever you want to put together a Software Teaming station quickly. It also works well for a permanent setup.

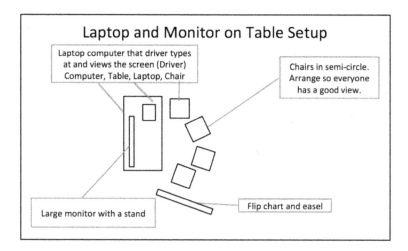

The Triangle Setup

This setup was devised for limited space. It uses three monitors with three keyboards. One or two people can sit at each monitor/keyboard station. It works well when you don't have a large monitor. As with the other setups, there's one computer, and the monitors mirror the same display.

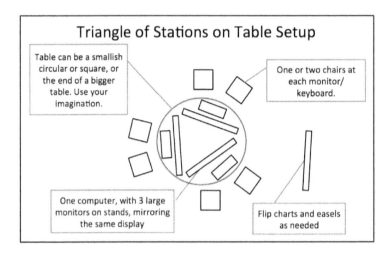

The Computer

There's only one computer used for programming and all the other work we do as a team. Individuals might use other computers for researching, examining databases, writing code snippets, writing emails, and other purposes in parallel with the team's work. There will often be more than one person searching for information about some problem or new technology we're trying to use. We all stay together and communicate continually about what we're learning.

Projectors or Monitors

A view with two projectors

Early on, we settled on a setup with two projectors that we use as dual monitors. Two monitors give us plenty of "real estate" to work with, so we can display several things simultaneously, such as our code, database tables, and internet searches. We project onto a wall with matte white paint formulated for projecting. After experimenting with height, distance, brightness, and other settings, we found a setup that works well for everyone on the team. We use identical, high-quality projectors. Each screen is projected at about four feet by six feet.

As we matured as a team, we replaced the projectors with large, high-quality monitors.

Keyboard/Mouse

There are two keyboards and two mice, so everyone has a choice that works for them. We experimented with several different keyboards and settled on two different setups (a "regular" one and a "natural" one). Some of our teams might use more than two keyboards. Each team can decide for themselves.

Hand sanitizer is always available.

Chairs and Tables

Each team member has their own high-quality chair adjusted for their own preferences. We move our chairs around as we take on the different roles (Driver or Navigators). This way, we don't need to readjust the chairs constantly.

Our work surface is two adjustable tables set to a comfortable height. We put the computer, keyboards/mice, projectors, phone, and speakers on the tables.

We also have rolling, magnetic whiteboards that we use for tracking our work and team discussions. In addition, there are easels, desk-height file cabinets, and other whiteboards.

Telephone and Email

All team-related telephone calls and email communications are done as a team. We sign our emails as "The Dev Team" and have a group email address. On phone calls, we specify that other team members are present. For example, "Hi Mary, this is Woody on speakerphone with a few other team members."

Ergonomics

We pay attention to ergonomic factors. We use natural keyboards and limit time at them. We can stand and change positions, limiting eye and back strain. We find that there's always more to learn about ergonomics, so we focus on it throughout the day. We cover more in the Ergonomics, Health, and Sanity chapter.

Private Work Area

We each have our own work areas to use whenever we desire. These small workspaces are in a separate annex to the Software Teaming area. These are configured as sit-down or stand-up, depending on individual preference, and with enough room for Pair Programming. Each work area has a computer, dual monitors, drawers, and a phone.

3 The Driver-Navigator Model In-Depth

Illustration © 2015 · Andrea Zuill

We have briefly discussed the Driver-Navigator model, but it's central to Software Teaming, so let's explore it in greater depth. In the Driver-Navigator model, there's one Driver, and the rest of the team are Navigators.

The essential point is that for an idea to go from someone's head into the computer, it must go through someone else's hands. This philosophy is so fundamental to Software Teaming that it bears repeating:

"For an idea to go from someone's head into the computer, it must go through someone else's hands."

Llewellyn Falco

Why is this idea so important? The main programming work is "thinking, describing, discussing, and steering" what we're developing. By having a separate typist, we gain an essential benefit: we discuss our design with everyone on the team. Everyone stays involved and informed. Typing is simply the mechanics of translating or transcribing ideas into code.

The Navigators and Navigation

The Navigators think, describe, discuss, and steer while the Driver translates. Navigating takes many forms and requires that team members become good at communicating, expressing ideas, questioning, and getting along well. The Driver-Navigator model provides a structure that makes sharing and expressing ideas easier. You may find other approaches that give you the same result.

The Navigators focus on the business logic of the current story, evolving the concepts and pursuing possible solutions. They articulate their intent, and when they see a promising path forward, they guide the Driver in coding.

If the Driver understands how to proceed, they can code the ideas without further direction. They can ask for clarification as needed, and each Driver might need a different level of navigation.

It's important to understand that Navigating isn't about "coding out loud." Instead, Navigating is about expressing intent and letting the Driver translate it into code.

We often use whiteboards, flip charts, or similar tools to aid in our discussion. Whiteboards provide a shared, temporary memory location for the team. The whiteboards reduce the need to repeat ourselves.

While the solution emerges, the Navigators focus on the next step(s) the team will take. This model prevents low-level coding details from distracting us from the high-level business problem we're solving.

It might seem like a group of Navigators expressing ideas could become a confusing mix of voices that a Driver can't follow. However, it's not a situation of everyone talking simultaneously. Instead, we take turns speaking. We pay attention to each other, listen to all ideas, suggest possible changes, and point out difficulties. In short, we learn to listen to each other, which is part of learning to treat each other with Kindness, Consideration, and Respect.

We follow ideas to their logical conclusion. We don't switch to a different idea until it's obvious we're ready for it. If there are multiple ideas, we try them all instead of debating which one to pursue.

The Driver and Driving

The keyboard is effectively a dumb input device, while the Driver is a smart input device that knows how to use the keyboard and write code. The Driver listens to guidance and ideas from the Navigators and translates them into code. Of course, being great at writing code is valuable, as well as knowing the languages, IDE, and tools, but the real work of software development is problem–solving, not typing.

If the Driver isn't highly skilled, the Navigators will help guide the Driver in creating the code, often suggesting keyboard shortcuts, language features, and Clean Code [1] practices. This guidance is a learning opportunity for the Driver, and we transfer knowledge quickly throughout the team, improving everyone's coding skills.

Everyone isn't required to take a turn at the keyboard as a Driver. Some team members aren't coders and don't feel comfortable trying to learn to code. For example, the product owner may not want to learn to write code. However, when we exercise a new feature, the product owner might want to take the Driver role. A person navigating might want to skip their turn driving if they're the best person to navigate the current task. To repeat, it's not a rule that everyone must take a turn as the Driver. It's up to the team to make everyone comfortable with their participation.

The Consultation and The Pause for Clarity

Software Teaming doesn't aim to produce a continuous conveyor belt of code. Sometimes, code entry must pause, and the team consults on where to go next. In these instances, we need to think and talk without coding.

A few examples of when a pause might be needed include

- We notice the solution we're trying isn't as useful as we hoped.
- We suspect we don't understand the problem we're trying to solve well enough to code it.
- The code is getting messy, and it's time to refactor.
- We feel stalled, blocked, or we're trying to code our way through something we don't understand.
- The solution isn't jumping out at us.
- We can't easily articulate the idea we're trying to code.
- We suspect we're heading down the wrong path.
- Anyone on the team thinks we need clarity or a pause.

The team can tune their approach by pausing, rethinking their solution, and exploring other possibilities. We often use the whiteboard to express ideas using diagrams or sketches during a pause. The goal is to contribute the right thing, at the right time, and in the right way. This goal improves the code, helping reveal the emerging design. We can get back to coding as soon as we have a clear path forward on a promising next step.

Note that we can't always discover a solution, so a pause doesn't always mean we will immediately find an answer. Sometimes we need to take time away from thinking, designing, or coding and let things incubate. Perhaps we can have lunch, take a walk, or work on something else, returning to it later. Often, a great solution will later appear.

Conflicting Ideas

There are usually many solutions for any particular programming challenge. When ideas are expressed, a conflict can arise when two programmers insist that their approach is the best and the team should adopt it. Conflicting views will occur, and we need to deal with them constructively.

With Software Teaming, we don't waste time deciding which of multiple ideas to try. We simply implement one, evaluate the result, and try another. This method allows ideas to morph, merge, evolve, and emerge. Sometimes we come up with an even better idea and try that one.

We don't allow conflicting views to turn into conflict that blocks us from moving forward. We simply try the ideas, learn from them, and act on what we learn. This approach means that everyone feels safe expressing their ideas without someone telling them, "that won't work."

An Example

So what does a Driver–Navigator team look like in action? See below. You can see the Navigators arrayed around the Driver working at the computer and translating the Navigators' ideas into code.

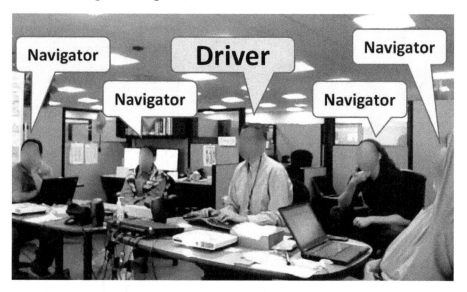

An example of the Driver-Navigator model in action

Rotating the Roles

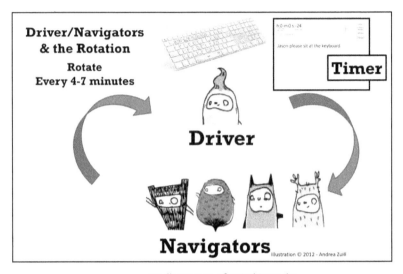

An illustration of switching roles

In the illustration above, we show an example of role rotation. But how does the role rotation actually work? Why do we switch the Driver? How often does the Software Teaming group switch to a new Driver? If we have someone really great at coding, shouldn't they stay at the keyboard? Let's take a look.

The How

We use a timer (more below) in our approach to rotation. As soon as the timer alerts us, the current Driver moves off the keyboard, and another Driver takes the keyboard according to a random rotation list created each morning.

We have used various rotation intervals, typically from four to fifteen minutes, with the current length being about seven minutes. We decrease the time when there are more people or someone new joins us. Rotation time can be whatever your team feels works best for them. What's optimal may be different for each team.

We used a timer, but this is just a holdover from our Coding Dojo practice. There's no strict rule to using a timer, and teams can choose whatever method they prefer for switching Drivers.

Please note that if you're driving and have an idea, hand the keyboard off and become a Navigator. Remember: for an idea to go from your head into the computer, it must go through someone else's hands.

The Why

At first, we simply followed the rotation model we used in our Coding Dojo. As we gained experience working this way, we found we liked taking turns. Everyone wanted to keep their hands in the code, which allowed the whole team to take part in the thinking and communicating. The Driver role frees the rest of the team to stay focused on the solution.

There's no rule that we must rotate the Driver in sorted order. The Driver can switch without a rotation schedule. For example, teams might prefer to keep the same Driver all day long, for the story's duration, or some different approach.

If you decide to switch Drivers frequently, it's important to do so quickly. Each Driver may have personal preferences regarding keyboard layout or editor setup. When the timer sounds, the current Driver simply moves their chair away from the keyboard, and the new Driver moves into place at the keyboard they prefer. The critical point is that the changeover should be quick and seamless.

A Timer

If the team decides to use a timer for Driver rotation, there are several things to consider. Each team will find what works best, but we'll mention a few things we tried.

For us, the timer's purpose was to help everyone stay engaged with the work. It made things lively and interesting.

At first, we just used the timer on someone's phone. It was easy to implement and told us exactly when to switch. However, it was too easy to ignore. A Driver would often say, "Hang on just a minute, let me finish this." We soon lost our rigor around changing the roles.

For our next timer, we tried one that was too loud to ignore. Unfortunately, it was so loud that it disturbed nearby teams, and it was still easy to ignore when the Driver wanted "just to finish this one thing."

Eventually, we wrote a simple timer program that hides the whole screen and asks the next person in the rotation to become the Driver. With this approach, we couldn't ignore the changeover, giving us a simple way to track who's next. Below is an early version of our timer.

An example timer program that blocks the screen

Summary

The Driver-Navigator model allows us to think through our ideas and better explain them before immediately putting them into code. This approach often produces more carefully designed code compared to rushing it into the computer.

As ideas are generated and translated into code, each idea is subject to other programmers' reviews. In effect, the design and code are continuously inspected, reviewed, and improved as it's created.

Programming is a challenging cognitive endeavor. It's difficult to stay mentally sharp and focused for long hours in front of a computer. As a result, fatigue occurs, and mistakes can slip in. It's easy for these to go unnoticed. We find that by spreading the cognitive load across more than one person, the Driver-Navigator model reduces the likelihood that fatigue will allow errors to creep in.

We believe there's a cognitive burden as we switch between problem, solution, and code. The Driver–Navigator model frees the Navigators of this cognitive overload, and perhaps we can perform each context at a deeper, more efficient level.

References

1. Martin, Robert C. Clean Code: A Handbook of Agile Software Craftsmanship. Pearson, 2008

4   Why Would We Work This Way?

It's a Trick Question

When we give presentations about Software Teaming at conferences and user groups, we'll ask the audience their thoughts on this question: Why would we work this way? But it's a bit of a trick question.

The Typical Answers

Here are some of the answers we commonly get about the possible benefits of working well together as a team.

- Continuous sharing and learning.
- Lots of brainpower on a single problem leads to better solutions.
- Continuous design and code review.

- It's fun.
- Less stress.
- Things get done and into Production sooner.
- We don't delay doing the things that produce Clean Code.

While these are excellent benefits, it doesn't answer the question, "Why would we work this way?"

The Real Answer: We Work this Way Because the Team Decided to Work this Way

This answer gets to a critical concept: the people doing the work can best decide how to do that work.

> *The people doing the work can best decide how to do that work.*

When hiring staff for software development work, we choose brilliant, capable, and motivated people who are accomplished in their lives and careers. And yet, in many organizations, we think we must "manage them." This method might work in some situations, but we think it's much less effective than we imagine.

Each team operates in its own context. Everything constantly changes, and we must adjust and steer as we go. There's no rulebook telling us what to do and how. There's no "one right way." Instead, there are endless possible right ways. We must discover as we go.

The only people close enough to the work context to adjust and steer as needed are the people doing the work. They alone have up-to-the-minute information and knowledge. They have the experience, skills, understanding, and ability to discover the approach needed to do the work.

Provide a Safe Place Where We can Discover Awesomeness

We must find a way to provide an environment where we release the natural awesomeness of each individual. When this exists, great things will happen.

We chose to work this way as a Software Teaming group because we saw many benefits. But we couldn't have done it without an environment where we could freely make that choice.

No one stopped us as we sought to Turn up the Good in everything we did. While a few people questioned what we were doing, the results were undeniably good.

We can't accomplish the great things we hope to achieve unless we allow those doing the work to create the workplace, practices, techniques, and approaches they need.

> *Let's learn to imagine how awesome things might be and then take a step in that direction.*

5   How Can We Work This Way?

Illustration © 2014 · Andrea Zuill

Working Together Isn't Always Easy

We often hear this when we first introduce Software Teaming: "An entire group of programmers trying to code something simultaneously? How can this possibly work? Programmers are forever arguing with each other about how to do things. As a group, how can we ever agree on how to code something or find a solution for a customer's need?"

Another thing we hear is, "We must separate our programmers so they don't argue with each other all day."

Working as a team all day, every day, means we spend a lot more time interacting with each other than we usually would. To make this work, we must consider how we treat each other.

Working Together Can Be Trying

We noticed we were getting on each other's nerves after Software Teaming for several months. We held a retrospective to see if we could Turn Up the Good on working well together.

We felt it would be worthwhile to have a team agreement about how to treat each other. On sticky notes, we each wrote some one-word completions to this sentence: "How I want to be treated: _____." We posted the notes on the wall and grouped them into themes. We then voted on the groupings we liked the most.

From this, we discovered how we wanted to be treated.

Kindness, Consideration, and Respect

We discovered that we wanted to be treated with Kindness, Consideration, and Respect.

If our teammates want to be treated with Kindness, Consideration, and Respect, we each need to take responsibility for treating them in such a manner.

We agreed on several things:

- We will treat each other with Kindness, Consideration, and Respect.
- We would practice using this as a guideline for how we would treat each other.
- We would start by pretending to treat each other this way and see what happens.

Things improved quickly. After a short while, we adopted this as our core agreement. We became more open to feedback and adjusted our behaviors based on that feedback. We were gently helping each other become better people.

We looked up the meanings of the words we chose for our agreement, and here's how we use these words:

Kindness: Act in a kindly way. Be warm-hearted, gentle, and polite. Display a pleasant disposition to others. Show concern for others.

Consideration: Consider your team members' ideas. To do this, we need to be able to listen. To listen requires humility. Our own idea is only one possible way. We need to try the other ideas rather than simply finding reasons not to try them.

We also need to consider each others' feelings. Considering others' feelings is much more difficult than considering their ideas. We don't have easy answers for making this happen. We encourage everyone to explore it themselves.

Respect: Respect is like a diplomatic protocol. It's about allowing others to keep their self-esteem. We can disagree and still be respectful. Disagreements generate ideas, but those ideas can't flourish in a disrespectful environment.

> *When we learn how to treat each other well, we create a path toward better solutions.*

A story from Woody: Once we started treating each other with Kindness, Consideration, and Respect, I found that I became more mindful of how I treated others. I started paying a lot more attention to opportunities to treat others better. I believe I am now a better person than I was before we started following this team agreement.

My teammates were respectful to me in giving me feedback. For easy things, they could do it in "real-time" as it happened. For example, if I was too insistent on an idea I was expressing, someone else might notice and say, "Woody, I think we have the idea of what you would like. Let's see if there are some ideas from the others."

If it were a more personal thing, someone would ask for a few minutes of my time to talk away from the team and share what they noticed. For example, if I had cut somebody off in a conversation, they might say, "Woody, did you notice you weren't giving Tim a chance to talk? It seems you might have hurt his feelings, and perhaps you'll need to apologize to him."

I'm still not the person I would like to be, but I'm thankful for the years of working on a team where we all paid attention to helping each other become better people.

Part Three: A Few Other Things

Illustration © 2013 - Andrea Zuill

This part of the book addresses miscellaneous topics related to Software Teaming. We examine some common questions and look at concerns that often arise for individuals as they consider becoming part of a Software Teaming group. When you finish this section, you should have answers to some typical questions about Software Teaming.

1   Continuous Learning

Illustration © 2014 - Andrea Zuill

Software Teaming is a wonderful "Continuous Learning" environment. Learning is accelerated and amplified almost automatically.

Software Teaming emerged out of an environment where we focused on turning up the good of learning for the entire team. Not surprisingly, it turns out to provide a rich environment for learning.

Initially, our goal was to introduce agile topics, practices, and techniques that might be helpful as the team became agile. Study sessions are one way to do this. We also brought in outside trainers and bought books and online study materials.

One of the first things we did was to set aside time to study and practice together.

2   Study and Practice Together

Illustration © 2014 - Andrea Zuill

A big part of what we practice when we study together is collaboration. While we learn various technologies for our work, that isn't the most important thing. The important thing is that we learn how to work well together and collaborate.

> It's important that we learn how to work well together and how to collaborate.

When we study and practice together, we gain a connection with each other that's difficult to achieve otherwise. These connections transfer into our daily work and help build an effective and enjoyable work environment.

Still, learning new technologies and code skills is also important, and studying and practicing together amplifies our ability to do that. We get Software Teaming's advantages: we bring everything we each know to help each other learn.

We used practice exercises to learn new technologies and how to collaborate. Using exercises liberates us to focus on learning by removing the pressure of working on actual work. This approach makes it easier to experiment, try things, change direction and throw things away. We believe setting aside time to study and practice together is essential.

Friday Afternoon Practice

We already had regular group study and practice sessions before discovering Software Teaming. We would gather every Friday for several hours to learn Clean Code techniques, Test-Driven Development, Design Patterns, and other vital topics. We practiced using coding exercises and studying new technologies that were becoming important to us.

Our group study was always voluntary. Not everyone chose to participate at first, but everyone eventually joined. These practice sessions grew into our Software Teaming style of working.

An important goal of these sessions was to help each other improve our capabilities and skills. A side benefit was that we became better at sharing, teaching, and asking useful questions.

Software Teaming and Learning

In our everyday work, with everyone working together on the same thing simultaneously, we naturally accelerate and amplify our learning. As we watch each other code, we pick up keyboard shortcuts, coding techniques, and Clean Code practices. As we discuss possible solutions, we diagram them and think through them as a team. This collaboration exposes us to possibilities we might never have considered when working separately.

A story from Kevin: I consider myself an experienced user of spreadsheet programs, particularly Microsoft® Excel®. I have been working with such programs since the days of Lotus 123 on a DOS machine.

Because of my decades of experience, I thought I knew every Excel® shortcut. Imagine my surprise when, in the first few minutes of visiting Woody's original Software Teaming group, one of the programmers showed me a shortcut I never knew existed. I immediately began using it and realized how much I would quickly learn if I worked full-time in a Software Teaming group. I would have access to the knowledge of an entire group, which wouldn't happen if I worked alone.

Our Morning Hour of Learning

During our work, peripheral questions would arise. For example, someone might say, "This class doesn't seem cohesive," and someone unfamiliar with software cohesiveness might ask about it. While we wanted to answer the questions, we didn't want to distract ourselves from the work at hand.

We decided to try holding an hour-long learning session each morning to cover these questions. Whenever one arose, we added it to our "study questions" list for the next morning. At the day's end, we selected one item from the list. Someone would offer to lead the discussion the next day.

Each morning we would discuss the item and ensure we all understood it to the degree we wanted. This discussion could take a few minutes or sometimes the whole hour. We'd discuss as many topics as possible in our Morning Hour of Learning. The sessions worked very well by helping us advance our knowledge without work interruption.

Keep it Safe to Learn

Working in a group means we're vulnerable beyond what we typically experience in our work. We must allow everyone to keep their self-esteem when they make a mistake.

Let's make it easy and comfortable for everyone to work without fear of feeling exposed. We enhance learning when we safely learn from our mistakes.

> *Safety enhances our relationships and capabilities because we can freely and comfortably admit when we don't know and can ask for help.*

The Beginner's Mind

Often the least experienced person on the team has great ideas that no one else does. If we don't listen for this and encourage it, we will miss many learning opportunities for the team and the individual. Making it safe for less experienced programmers to share and try their ideas is critical to achieving the benefits of collaboration.

3   Exposed

Illustration © 2012 - Andrea Zuill

The Fear of Being Exposed

Working on a team where everything you do, every mistake, every slip, and every frailty is in full view isn't for everyone. We'll cover what this might mean to some people and what we can do about it.

Why It Might be Frightening

In Software Teaming, we work with others so that everyone sees almost everything we do. Many aspects of our personality, work habits, and technical abilities are visible. There's nowhere to hide. Some of us might not be able to deal with that.

Working in a group isn't easy for some people and might not come naturally. It's especially challenging for many of us in the software industry because we've usually worked alone our entire careers. Working in a group is a significant change. As a result, not everyone will feel comfortable doing this.

Some things can make Software Teaming scary for some people. We might wonder, "What happens if I make mistakes in front of everyone? What if everyone sees 'how little I know?' Is it safe to be so vulnerable in front of all my coworkers?" These can be tricky things to overcome.

What Can We do About It?

Agile and Software Teaming recognize the value of providing an environment where individuals can do well and work well together. If we make this our collective responsibility, the exposure will become less of a problem.

Some of us are afraid of being exposed, while some cause others to fear being exposed. We might not realize we're making others feel uncomfortable about their abilities. It's essential to understand this: we must learn to work well together.

Some people might never overcome the fear of exposure. It's not for everyone, and we think that's fine. With time and our teammates' help, some of us can overcome the fear and learn to enjoy Software Teaming. For some, this moment may never arrive. We need to understand that.

Mistakes are Part of the Process

Fear of punishment or ridicule for mistakes is at the heart of many things we're reluctant to try. Can we change our attitudes about them? There are techniques we can attempt.

Mistakes are essential parts of the learning and discovery process. Senior team members should make it clear that they make mistakes and not attempt to hide them. This openness helps the other team members learn that we all make mistakes and they're part of the process.

It's better if we own each other's mistakes by not believing "it's someone else's." It's our mistake.

Consider adopting a "No blame, no shame" mindset. Never blame others. Never shame them. In so doing, we create an open environment where learning is an inevitable byproduct.

Make it Voluntary

Much of the safety of a Software Teaming group comes from its voluntary nature. Allow everyone to participate in the manner they find most comfortable. That might mean only sometimes or never participating.

Conclusion

Being exposed can be frightening to some. It's an inherent characteristic of the Software Teaming approach. We can learn to deal with that by treating each other well, accepting mistakes as a learning tool, and making participation voluntary. Most importantly, let's understand that the fear of being exposed isn't necessarily an individual problem. Instead, it's something for the team to address.

4 Ergonomics, Health, and Sanity

Illustration © 2013 · Andrea Zuill

Let's Take Care of Ourselves

Staying healthy doesn't happen automatically. We'll cover a few things we've discovered about keeping ourselves free from sickness, injury, and insanity.

When we started Software Teaming, we didn't pay much attention to these things. However, as we noticed various problems (sore necks, headaches, and feeling drowsy after lunch), we set about finding ways to change our environment and behaviors to help lessen them.

Projectors, Chairs, Keyboards, and Screens

One of the first things we noticed was that we were getting sore necks. We sat at a conference table with the projector at one end, requiring us to turn our heads to see the screen. Another thing we noticed was some of us squinting to see the work. The fonts were too small, the contrast wasn't correct, or the colors weren't ideal.

We also found that the meeting rooms' chairs weren't meant for an entire day of sitting. They were fine for a typical hour-long meeting, but we were getting sore backs and legs from sitting in them all day. They were uncomfortable and not easily adjusted.

We soon moved to our first permanent space, giving us control over our environment. Here are some things we found that helped eliminate many problems.

- Use large, high-quality monitors. Finding ones that make reading easy without straining our eyes is crucial.
- Use the proper height of the monitor screen. Most meeting room screens are too high for all-day use, requiring that we tilt our heads up to see.
- Adjust the font sizes, colors, and other settings to ensure everyone can comfortably read the code and other documents without squinting.
- Sit a proper distance from the monitors.
- Orient our bodies to face the monitors so we don't have to crane our necks.
- Use proper posture when sitting.
- Stand frequently.
- Use good quality chairs. Each person should have their own chair selected for an ergonomic fit and adjusted to their preference. We mark the chairs and use only our own, so the adjustments stay set for their owner.
- Provide a selection of keyboards so everyone can use one that suits their needs. While we generally type less than solo programmers, repetitive stress disorders are still possible.
- Use a proper table height. Ideally, we should have a table with an adjustable height to suit the Driver.

Stretching, Taking Walks, Taking Breaks

Early on, we noticed several team members taking walks at lunch. They were enjoying it, and soon, we all joined, helping us stay more alert and focused after lunch.

Additionally, we stretched twice a day, once in the midmorning and once in the afternoon. This practice helped us stay fit, alert, and healthy. We used stretches from our company's fitness coaches.

Each individual was allowed to take breaks whenever they wanted. We also would often take breaks as a group.

Preventing the Spread of Illness

We made liberal use of hand sanitizer before each keyboard use. This practice makes it less likely to spread illness by sharing a keyboard.

We sat far apart to avoid sneezing and coughing on each other, reducing the likelihood of spreading illness. It also gave us the added comfort of personal space.

For many of us, it can be tempting to "hang in there" when sick because we want to demonstrate our team dedication. Unfortunately, this can result in spreading illness. It may also lengthen our convalescence. When in doubt, it's best to be cautious and take care of ourselves. Anyone would leave as soon as it was clear they weren't feeling well. We can always choose to join the team remotely if we're well enough.

Sanity

At first, it isn't always easy to work together all day, every day, with a team of others. As programmers, we're probably used to working alone most of the day. A few simple guidelines will help us maintain our sanity and enjoy working with our colleagues daily.

- Treat each other with Kindness, Consideration, and Respect. Put simply: treat others the way they would like to be treated.
- Maintain a relaxed and sustainable pace. The details are in the upcoming "Relaxed and Sustainable" chapter. We can summarize it as: you don't have to be a hero. There's no need to be on the leading edge of all discussions. It's more sustainable to relax, take mental "breaks," and give others a chance to be involved.

5 Retrospectives: Reflect, Tune, and Adjust Frequently

Illustration © 2013 - Andrea Zuill

If You Only Have Time to Get Good at One Thing, Start with Retrospectives

What's the most important "Agile Practice?" Perhaps it's to have regular Retrospectives. Learning how to get good results from retrospectives is well worth the effort.

This one idea has been powerful in our progress to make things better. This topic is worth its own book, but we'll keep it short and explore some important and useful concepts.

The idea is this: examine how things are going, decide on something to make better, decide on an action to take, take action, and reflect on it. Then repeat the whole thing sometime soon.

The Daily Retrospective

At first, we held retrospectives about every two weeks. We picked something to improve and spent the next two weeks trying to make the improvements. While this worked well, we sensed it was too long between sessions.

Sometimes when an issue comes to our attention, it might be better to address it immediately rather than wait for two weeks. Why wait when we can make improvements now?

We decided to meet more frequently and eventually started holding a concise retrospective at the end of each day. These short but frequent retrospectives dramatically "turned up the good." This approach is like "continuous delivery" but for process improvements. We deliver improvements daily and use the feedback to steer us to the next step.

Another practice we discovered is the "just-in-time" retrospective. Whenever a team member would notice anything important, insightful, or surprising, we would hold an "instant retrospective." It's beneficial to reflect on something while the experience is fresh in our minds.

As a team, we liked to use retrospectives to reflect, tune and adjust every chance we got. The more retrospectives we did, the better our team performed.

We'll cover more about the Daily and Just-In-Time retrospectives in the upcoming Turn Up The Good chapter. The rest of this chapter covers how we used retrospectives to improve things.

An Example of a Typical Retrospective

As an example of one way we use retrospectives, we'll share a series of retrospectives we did and describe how we used them to make improvements.

In this case, we used the "Affinity Mapping" approach, where we each write down our ideas on sticky notes, one idea per note. We put them on the wall and sort them into groupings of similar ideas. The resulting affinity map shows us where we have common themes to focus on.

Here are the sticky notes and affinity mappings for four retrospectives.

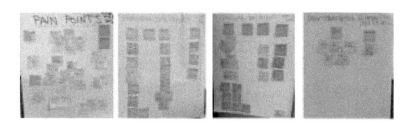

An Affinity Mapping Example

In our first retrospective in this series, we identified several areas we wanted to improve. Here's one group from the mapping exercise we decided to work on.

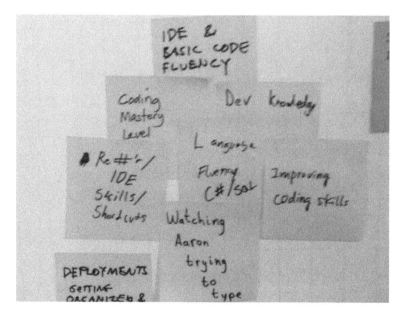

The items include:

- Code fluency
- Coding skills

- IDE skills
- Typing skills
- Programming language fluency
- Resharper Skills
- Shortcuts

Give it a Name

When an affinity mapping gathers enough sticky notes to show we have an area of common interest, we try to develop a name for it. This one was easy to name: Developer Skills.

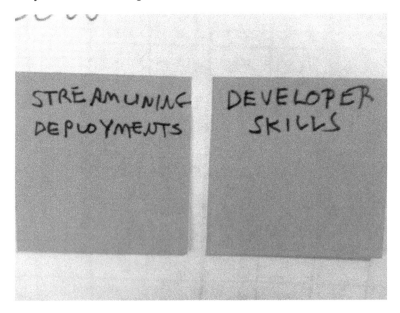

We always discuss the things we discover during a retrospective and try to find an action we can take. In this case, we decided to take time to think and meet later to discuss how to proceed. We're flexible. Remember, no practice is written in stone. (Except for DO RETROSPECTIVES. That actually IS written in stone.)

We held a "Lean Coffee" style meeting when we gathered again. This meeting style involves everyone suggesting topics, writing them on sticky notes, prioritizing them, and discussing them in prioritized order. We spend a few minutes per item until we have enough ideas to discuss. In this example, we created ideas for improving our developer skills. Some ideas seemed to fit together naturally, so we grouped them and soon had a few things to try, as shown below.

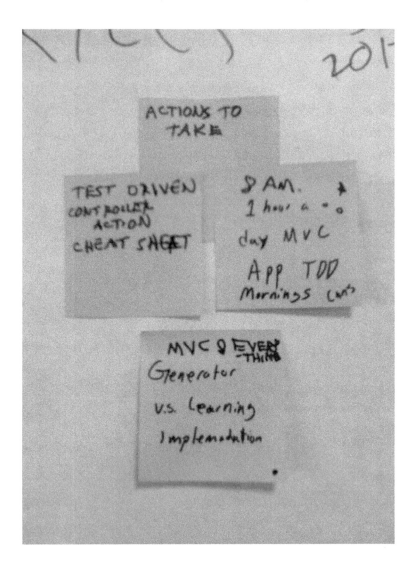

- Create a "cheat sheet" or "checklist" for the steps for some everyday tasks.
- Review and learn the motivations behind our code generator.

- Hold a daily one-hour practice period focusing on Model-View-Controller, Test-Driven-Development, and basic coding skills.

A Daily Practice Period

Holding daily practice periods seems like something we should have done from the start. We talked about it for a year, but sometimes that's how it is with good ideas. They're stuck on the back burner until they've simmered just enough, and then we move them to the front.

We were doing a weekly study and practice period, which was very beneficial. So in the spirit of Extreme Programming, we decided to Turn up the Good and try adding an hour-long daily practice period. To ensure that we were "Turning up the Good," we kept the more extended weekly practice session in addition to the daily sessions.

We've long been using the "practice" of daily practice. Almost every morning, we practice a coding activity. We've refined it over time, but the basic idea has stayed the same.

Another Retrospective, Another Step Forward: The Twelve Days of Index

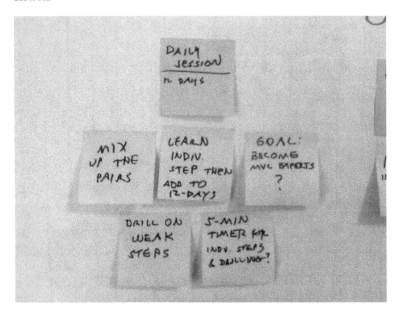

After some time, we held another retrospective of our practice sessions. Although things were very positive, we noticed we weren't gaining mastery over something we practiced: creating an index controller and its related parts and tests.

We discussed our approach and a few ideas to try. One method we adopted is similar to how I (Woody) used to practice the banjo when I was first learning (many, many years ago):

- Practice a little bit of a tune you want to learn (just a measure or two).
- Once you have that down, learn the following little bit in isolation from the part you just learned.

- Once you master that, combine it with the part you already learned, and practice those together until it flows nicely.
- If the transition from the first to the second part gives you trouble, isolate and practice the transition.
- Once the "combined parts" work well, learn the next little bit, then combine.

We gave this "practice of practicing" a name: "The Twelve Days of ..." (fill in the .... with the name of the thing to practice). It's a little like the song "The Twelve Days of Christmas." You sing the first part alone, then the second AND the first part, then the third AND the second AND the first part. In this case, we practiced coding an index controller, so we called it "The Twelve Days of Index."

The concept is to master each small part "in order," adding the result to what we have already mastered. Everything is learned "in the small" and builds to encompass the whole concept we want to learn. It works quite well.

Things to Notice

- We pay attention to figure out what needs attention.
- We experiment and try things that might lead to improvement.
- We review and make changes as often as needed.
- We name things in a way that makes it easy to "get the idea" and talk about what we do.
- We practice doing the work we do.
- As we become better at a practice, we look for ways to improve that practice.

The Takeaway

It's helpful to be good at retrospectives, and it's even more beneficial to be good at getting good results from the retrospectives. In effect, we found it helpful to Turn up the Good on "turning up the good." The result was that our retrospectives became much more beneficial to us.

> *Book suggestion*: There's an excellent book on the subject: "*Agile Retrospectives: Making Good Teams Great*" by Diana Larsen and Esther Derby. We've worn out the first copy of the book. We ordered new copies of the book, and a workgroup meets weekly to practice the book's ideas and techniques. In other words, we now retrospect on our retrospectives and practice getting better at it.

6   Turn Up the Good

Illustration © 2020 - Andrea Zuill

Something that Works Well: Turn Up the Good

"Turning up the good" comes from Kent Beck and Extreme Programming. The idea is to pay attention to what works well and find a way to make it even better.

"When I first articulated XP, I had the mental image of knobs on a control board. Each knob was a practice that, from experience, I knew worked well. I would turn all the knobs up to ten and see what happened. I was a little surprised to find that the whole package of practices was stable, predictable, and flexible."

Kent Beck

This philosophy is a profoundly different way of thinking about how we do our work.

What's Wrong with Solving Problems?

There's nothing wrong with solving problems. We rightly focus on things that aren't working and should be fixed. This strategy is very effective, and there's no reason to abandon it. When something needs to be fixed, then let's fix it.

But what if we ask, "What's already good, and can we get more of it?" It's deceptively simple: notice what's working well, and find a way to turn it up.

Turning up the good isn't about solving problems. It's about accentuating the things that are going well. We amplify any nuance of goodness that we notice.

Noticing the Hint of Goodness Whenever We Can

It isn't always natural to look for the good and bring it to the fore. It takes the conscious practice of paying attention to anything different. Capture, ponder, and reflect on anything with a faint glimmer of goodness. Mention it out loud, "Did you notice that? How can we get more of that next time?" We start seeing the good in everything as we get good at this.

Exploring Ways to Turn it Up

Once we've discovered something good that we think is worth turning up (and most of it is), we can start exploring the possibilities.

It's been helpful for us to ask "what" questions, such as:

- "What would it be like if ...?"
- "What would it take to ...?"
- "What would have to be true for ...?"

Here's an obvious and relevant example:

"We noticed that working together during this meeting was good. What would it be like if we worked this way all day long? What would it take to make it easy to do that? What would have to be true for us to want to continue doing this?"

Being Resolute in Searching for the Pocket of Goodness

The busyness of work often distracts us from following up on little things that might be good if we had a chance to grow and mature them. It can be easy to let things drop. Watch for this and find ways to keep the good things in mind, so they don't wither.

Make it a habit to look for good every day and reflect on it at the day's end. Doing this makes it almost automatic to uncover the good and turn it up.

When you find something good, make it visible. Put it where the whole team can see it. Refer to it regularly. "These are the good things we've been noticing" and "Here are the things we've been trying." Take time to review the ideas and concepts emerging from this collection of goodness.

> *Notice what works well, and find a way to turn it up.*

Noticing goodness is one of our most crucial actions to create effective teams. It's a potent form of continuous improvement.

Nurture and Grow the Goodness

Emerging goodness requires protection from things that can devour goodness before it becomes established. It requires conscious effort to be protected.

"Protect new ideas from those who don't understand that for greatness to emerge, there must be phases of not-so-greatness."

Ed Catmull

---

7 Relaxed and Sustainable

Illustration © 2007 - Andrea Zuill

This is Wearing Us Out!

Once others started Software Teaming worldwide, we often heard from folks who remarked that they found it fatiguing. For them, the amount of concentration, interaction, and focus without having a minute to relax was something they could only handle for a few hours a day.

We weren't experiencing this on our team, so we started investigating. We had been practicing working well together for months before we began Software Teaming. We had learned how to explain our ideas clearly, let others express themselves without interruption, and patiently try other people's ideas.

The Fatigue Problem

Fatigue may occur because people fear they'll miss something if they don't pay attention every second. Maybe they feel they must constantly contribute or share their ideas about everything happening. Sometimes we might think we let down our team if we don't help every minute. Perhaps we feel we aren't working hard if we don't always contribute.

We Don't Need to Be a Hero

Working as a team can lessen the need for intense focus because it spreads the load across the group. An important idea comes from the book "*Essentialism: The Disciplined Pursuit of Less*" by Greg McKeown [1]:

"We aren't looking for a plethora of good things to do. We are looking for our highest level of contribution: the right thing the right way at the right time."

Greg McKeown

In other words, we don't have to contribute all the time but only when our contribution seems appropriate and timely. It would be rare that each person must discuss every possibility, find every objection, or even fully pay attention at every moment.

There are likely times when our help actually might not be helpful. Sometimes it's better just to let things unfold while quietly observing. If it becomes clear that our contribution is needed, then that's the right time to offer it. People will ask for your help when they feel they need it.

We can't boil this down into a simple algorithm of when to speak and when to remain silent. It comes with practice and patience. It might be helpful to think of it as a dance of ideas with its own rhythm where people step in and step out as appropriate.

In a sense, Software Teaming is a "Cognitive Collective." We gather everyone's brain and use their cognitive powers to augment the individual's abilities. As with any team, the whole is more powerful than the individual. Sometimes, one individual lags, but the team picks up the slack. Conversely, there will be times when the team lags, but an individual picks up the slack. And occasionally, a cognitive whirlwind forms, which draws everyone to participate and contribute.

Sometimes the hero isn't the action figure. Sometimes the hero is the person that lets others speak and contribute.

Taking an Individual Break

Sometimes we might need a break, and there's no reason the team can't continue working when an individual is getting coffee or relaxing for a moment. We all need to catch our breath. The work is a marathon, not a sprint. When a team member thinks there's something important they need from you, they'll ask.

The context of our work changes over time, but stepping away for a few minutes won't cause us to lose the overall context. It only takes a few moments to catch up with everyone else.

We've even found that vacationing for a week or more isn't a problem. Everyone else keeps working while we're away. What the team learns in the interim is discoverable upon our return. This approach provides a very fluid arrangement as we dynamically adjust to the natural flow of our lives.

Sometimes the whole team takes a break together, but more commonly, each member takes breaks whenever they feel they need one.

Make it Sustainable

While maintaining a sustainable pace on the team, we must also keep a sustainable pace over the longer term. That means getting sufficient rest and time away from work to remain refreshed, alert, and clearheaded.

> *A story from Woody*: Work just enough. Whatever the "normal" workday is, follow that. Eight hours total time at work is what we've done. I recall we stayed late only once in the four years I worked with the original Software Teaming group.
>
> While we had no work hours rules, we naturally aligned to come in at 8:00 am, take an hour for lunch at noon, and leave at 5:00 pm.
>
> Everyone on the team has a life outside of work. This way, they have time to be with their family, do their hobbies, get sufficient sleep, take care of their personal life, and still come to work rested, refreshed, and alert, ready to contribute the right thing at the right time in the right way.

If you're exhausted, allow yourself to step back and take a break, returning to the team once you're rested, refreshed, and focused. Reflect on why you're becoming exhausted and take steps to eliminate that. It's even better to take breaks before you're tired. We can't give our best unless we're working in a relaxed and sustainable manner.

> *It's not about getting the most work out of each person. It's about getting the best of everyone into everything we do.*

References

1. McKeown, Greg. Essentialism: The Disciplined Pursuit of Less, Crown Business, 2014.

8 Barriers to Software Teaming

Illustration © 2012 - Andrea Zuill

We often see barriers to Software Teaming that prevent or slow its adoption. The following list is by no means exhaustive but addresses some of the common roadblocks that often arise.

The System Resists Change

Ask any organization's management team if they're innovative, and you'll probably get answers like, "We are innovative and seek those who think outside the box."

Except it sometimes isn't true.

Software Teaming means innovation for most organizations. Innovation means change, and change is something that may or may not produce satisfactory results. It's unknowable until after the change is implemented. If the result is unsatisfactory, we can't recover the time and money. The uncertainty of how change plays out means that organizations sometimes resist it—usually unknowingly but occasionally consciously. If an organization's history includes an innovation that went wrong, then the anxiety of unpredictable change is coupled with the wounds of a prior failure. Combined, these produce a barrier to change.

More importantly, compensation structures often incentivize maintaining the status quo of the existing system while innovation seeks to disrupt it. This conflict lies at the heart of the difficulty in implementing change.

Finally, no matter how well-intentioned, the moment a policy is enacted, a constituency is born whose livelihood depends on perpetuating the policy. The takeaway is to be extremely careful with instituting policies because they too often transform from *"them serving us"* to *"we serving them."*

> *No matter how innocent and well-intentioned, the moment a policy is enacted, a constituency is born whose livelihood depends on perpetuating the policy.*

Merge all these factors, and it's no surprise when an entrenched system resists when confronted with innovation. The irony, of course, is that while an organization may fight internal change, it's perpetually subject to external change. If it can't find a way to reconcile these two opposing forces, it will eventually succumb to the external pressures that destroy its business model.

"It is not necessary to change. Survival is not mandatory."

W. Edwards Deming

What are we to do when confronted with this resistance?

Work with stakeholders to change the system while understanding that it can sometimes be a frustrating and fruitless struggle. Regardless of the outcome, it's beneficial to adopt the attitude that we'll learn something along the way. If the skills we gain aren't valuable for the current environment, they'll potentially be helpful in future ones.

It also helps to realize that these forces are intrinsic to all organizations. Some organizations manifest them worse than others, but few are entirely immune. The larger and more established a company is, the more likely it is to be affected, primarily if it employs a top-down, command-and-control philosophy. But startups don't always escape these forces either. Those most immune are organizations that prize local decision-making, a hallmark of Agility.

A story from Kevin: Many years ago, I was a new middle manager in a software company undergoing training in managing according to the company's dictates. We trainees spent an entire week at an offsite facility. We worked hard to understand such things as listening to our direct reports and helping them drive change in our organization.

One of the things that had become clear to me was that Research and Development (R&D) was essential but not being done. I had this thought in mind when, on the final day, we trainees were granted a visit from our CEO, who was there to congratulate us and present us with our management certificates.

During an open Question-and-Answer session with the CEO, I excitedly asked if we could innovate by committing to an R&D endeavor. Surprisingly, the CEO cut me off before I could finish and told me loudly, "No, you're wrong. We tried that once, and it didn't work. We wasted a lot of money on it and aren't doing it again. Next question."

Equally surprising to me was the reaction of all the management trainers who had just spent an entire week instructing us on the importance of listening to our employees. They fell silent, and we quickly moved on to the next question.

Years later, I realized that this experience was my first lesson in how systems resist change and how those pursuing innovation sometimes face a difficult job, even when tasked with it.

Our Manager Won't Let Us

When proposing Software Teaming, it's not uncommon for managers to reject it. This is an understandable first reaction. Here are some options.

Take baby steps. Try it as a small-scale experiment. You can start with a small team for a few hours per week. Freely share what you're learning.

Use Software Teaming as a study group for learning a new technology everyone needs to know.

To help make the case, review The Power of Flow and Problems That Faded Away chapters. They point out that Software Teaming has been a practical and effective approach for us. If costs are the manager's concern, review the chapter Won't This Cost Too Much?

It helps to understand that Software Teaming may be too much change for some organizations to accept at first. Attitudes might evolve with time and enough experiments to show Software Teaming's effectiveness.

We Don't Have a Space to Do It

That's OK. Start with any available open space. Improvise to make something work. See the Workspace Setup and Quick Start Guide chapters for ideas on how to set things up.

We Don't Know How to Get Started

It can be overwhelming at first. Review the Quick Start Guide chapter and take small steps to get moving. You don't need to start with a Big Bang approach.

Our Teams Don't Even Want to Pair Program

While similar, Software Teaming and Pair Programming are different in some ways. Software Teaming is a much more social approach. It provides a "safety in numbers" you don't get with Pair Programming.

We've noticed that many teams have quickly adopted Software Teaming even though they were initially reluctant to Pair Program. Remember, we've found it's better if participation is voluntary. Start with those interested, and perhaps others will gain interest with time.

The Tech Lead Coded While Everyone Watched

This isn't uncommon. It stems from a natural desire to be helpful. Remember: For an idea to go from someone's head into the computer, it must go through someone else's hands. If the coding knowledge lies with the Tech Lead, then that person should be one of the Navigators.

It may be beneficial to read the Driver–Navigator In–Depth chapter. Also, try to treat each other with Kindness, Consideration, and Respect.

We Were Exhausted After a Few Hours

Exhaustion happens when everyone feels they must always contribute to their utmost at all times. The result is often exhaustion, making it hard to continue. Remember, there's no need to be a hero. It's OK to take a breather and stay fresh. Read the chapter Relaxed and Sustainable for more ideas.

We Aren't Really Very Agile.

What if our organization isn't well-versed in Agile methods or isn't yet practicing many of them? What if there's no Test Driven Development, Continuous Delivery, Retrospectives, etc.?

Software Teaming is an excellent method to learn these things. It's easier to understand them as a group than on your own. Try them as Software Teaming exercises.

9 Won't This Cost Too Much?

Illustration © 2012 · Andrea Zuill

Is This Cost-Effective?

At first glance, Software Teaming seems like it would be a costly way to develop software. After all, when we work independently, we surely get multiple things done simultaneously. And if we group people to work together simultaneously, we surely get only one thing done. Anyone can see that more things done are better than one thing done. Indeed, when first proposing Software Teaming to managers, we often hear these responses.

"I'm not paying five people to do the work of one."

"I want to get five things done, not just one."

It's simple math, right? We don't think so. We believe it isn't that simple, and the math isn't so linear or straightforward.

Before we see why let's get straight to the disclaimer: to date, no controlled scientific experiments prove Software Teaming is a cheaper way to produce better quality software. There are also no studies that demonstrate the reverse either: that solo programming is cheaper than

Software Teaming. It would be the same study. We rarely hear someone question the practice of solo programming while questioning Software Teaming.

There are numerous studies on Pair Programming, and most of them generally suggest a benefit to pairing, though some show a drawback. Given the number of variables involved and the different approaches to measuring them, it isn't surprising that there are differing conclusions [1], [4], [5], [6], [7].

So that brings us to empirical evidence, which isn't rigorous. But we can still draw some conclusions from our experience with Software Teaming. Let's examine these individually.

The Myth of Getting Multiple Things Done Simultaneously

Do we simultaneously get multiple things done when we separate workers? We don't think so. We believe separating workers entails considerable costs that aren't obvious unless we look for them.

For starters, it's common to find that many separated tasks contain dependencies on each other. These dependencies mean that some tasks only can be completed after others are finished, immediately reducing the amount of work done in parallel. Worse, while waiting on a task to finish, workers are often told, "find something else to work on," thereby creating costly queues, inventory, and context-switching.

Next, we can only achieve parallelism if each team member has all the required knowledge to perform their work. If this isn't true, team members must interrupt each other's work to ask for help. This further reduces the amount of work done in parallel and causes additional context-switching.

We also must consider the delays associated with coordinating the work of separated individuals. Time must be wasted on emails, phone calls, meetings, and other activities for everyone to be aligned on their tasks. Work isn't getting done if we're in meetings, further reducing our parallelism.

We often perform requirements discovery up front, believing it avoids the delays of work coordination. However, we can only discover requirements once we begin the work. Spending time defining them up front means we'll find their shortcomings downstream. Once we encounter problems, we're back to emails, phone calls, and meetings to sort them out. We aren't doing parallel work when this happens.

These barriers mean that what seems to be parallel work on paper often becomes anything but. Our experience has been that "getting multiple things done simultaneously" becomes a sequence of start-stop actions that take much longer than anticipated because they aren't genuinely parallel.

We think that when we separate workers to achieve parallel work, we aren't "getting a lot of things done." We're actually just "working on a lot of things" that take longer to achieve because we're working separately.

The Cost of Onboarding

Though it's rarely a line item on budgets, there's an unavoidable cost to onboarding a new hire. The new employee requires considerable time to learn the code, business logic, and numerous deployment tools and protocols.

It may be months before a new hire can fully contribute to complex software without oversight or assistance. Meanwhile, this assistance must come from other workers, reducing their output.

In short, there's a long period before the investment in a new hire pays off. Making the situation worse, some managers might expect new hires to quickly come up to speed without draining time from their coworkers. This situation creates poorly-trained workers who deploy defective software into Production.

As we see it, this cost is reduced with Software Teaming. On the new worker's first day, they're immediately immersed in the environment's intricacies and protocols. But they're not alone. They're safely working alongside their teammates.

They can offer their technical knowledge knowing their teammates will prevent them from blundering into a business logic error. They quickly learn the low-level details of checking in code and building and deploying it. Our experience has been that our new hires often begin delivering value almost immediately. This rapid onboarding saves us time and money.

Single Point of Failure

Many organizations have a programmer with all the knowledge of how the system works. Or perhaps only they understand a particularly complicated module. Managers fear this crucial person will someday quit or become gravely ill, throwing the company into turmoil and possibly causing irreparable harm. Occasionally, this key person is fully aware of their importance and hoards information to increase their perceived value to the company.

This single point of failure causes a risk to the company's long-term survival. Our experience is that this risk is an unavoidable outgrowth of separating the workers and that this separation inevitably produces knowledge silos. We believe these are costly risks for any organization.

As we see it, Software Teaming's "whole team together" approach prevents the costly introduction of knowledge silos. We find that knowledge is disseminated quickly among the team. Information is never hoarded with this style of collaboration because it's shared with everyone the moment it becomes available. We think there's a benefit to removing the hidden costs of single points of failure.

The Cost of Defects

Separating workers makes it more challenging to include design and code reviews in our daily work. Reviews are the foundation of creating quality code that's easy to maintain and update. When working separately, we must schedule reviews and inspect the code line-by-line. These reviews happen after the code is written, which is costly because we often must rework the completed code.

When schedules become tight, as they usually are, it's easy to skip the reviews altogether. A lack of reviews often causes poor code to enter the system. And poor code is costly to maintain because it's typically filled with defects.

Defects are usually born in the darkness of solo work. Our experience is that defects are reduced when we bring code into the sunlight, where a Software Teaming group carefully reviews it in real-time.

How costly are defects? Estimates vary, but they're expensive. They're typically a significant technical expense encountered when constructing software.

Let's see an example of this cost by using industry statistics to perform a simple calculation. An experienced programmer writes about 25 lines of code (LOC) per hour [1]. (There are well-documented problems with any LOC metric [2], but it will do for our simple analysis.) According to Williams [1], the average number of defects injected per thousand lines of code (KLOC) is 39. Therefore, a single hour of coding will inject 0.975 defects (25/1000*39). There's a 15% chance that a defect will escape to Production [1]. If it does, it typically requires 33 hours to repair [1]. That means it could require about

4.8 hours (0.975*0.15*33) to fix the defects from a single hour of coding, far more than it took to write it. Even if we assume that it takes only 10% of the 33 hours to repair a Production defect, that's still about 30 minutes, one-half the time to write the code. These are very high costs.

We can quibble with the numbers, but there's no reasonable way to manipulate them into making the costs inconsequential. Indeed, the values used are conservative, given that some studies show defect rates are much higher than stated here [3]. The inescapable conclusion is that defects are frightfully expensive. Anything we can do to reduce their quantity is money well spent.

We believe we achieve cost savings on defect repair when implementing Software Teaming. According to Williams [1], Pair Programming produces 40% of the defects of a solo programmer. It seems reasonable to assume that the multiple reviewers of a Software Teaming group will further reduce that. The defect rate could be much lower because, according to Rico [4], Pair Programming produces only 6% of the defects of solo programmers.

All this said, we have no rigorous studies proving that Software Teaming reduces defect rates, and it certainly isn't foolproof enough to eliminate all defects. But we have empirical evidence of defect rates plummeting when we began Software Teaming.

Somewhat surprisingly, we find that some companies view defects as an annoyance instead of a costly drain on finances, whereas our philosophy is to reduce them as much as possible.

We know of one company doing Software Teaming where teams typically go months—and sometimes years—without a bug reported, even with multiple daily Production deployments. Indeed, defects at this company are so rare that there's no longer any need for a bug database. We attribute this to having many eyes reviewing designs and code in real-time. We think it's easy to make mistakes when working solo but less likely when everyone is watching for errors.

The Cost of Delayed Testing

When we work separately, we usually perform final testing only after everyone's code is finished. Waiting until everyone finishes means problems aren't discovered until the testing phase.

The testing phase is usually our first glimpse into everyone's interpretation of the requirements. It's here that we often discover there are misunderstandings about what's needed. If there are dependencies between each person's code, a misunderstanding in one area can affect numerous others.

The testing phase is also the first time stakeholders can see their features in action. Upon seeing them, they sometimes realize that features should behave differently than they initially imagined and must be changed.

These problems mean that code must be reworked and retested in a costly, time-consuming loop until the issues are resolved. Many organizations accept this rework as just another task in software development without realizing its actual cost.

In our experience of Software Teaming, there's little need for repeated rounds of "test-fix-test." Everyone, including testers, works together at the same time and on the same computer. We share a common definition of the problem we're solving, so there are no misunderstandings scattered across separated workers. We work on one small piece at a time and test it as soon as it's coded, minimizing the rework cycle. What we learn from this one piece informs what we need for the next small piece, allowing us to steer toward a solution in small increments.

We believe that we achieve significant cost savings as a result.

The Cost Savings from Problems that Faded Away

Many problems resulting from working separately faded away when we started Software Teaming. Here is a partial list of those problems (see Problems that Faded Away for more detail).

- Faulty Communications
- Issues with Decision Making
- Doing More than What is Barely Sufficient
- Thrashing
- Politics
- Meetings

When we work separately, these items create costs because they represent time not spent creating software. These costs can often be substantial, but we rarely display them as line items in our budgets. Instead, they're usually considered an inevitable cost of doing business—if we stop to consider their costs at all.

Our experience with Software Teaming has been that when these problems faded away, so did their hidden costs, allowing us to spend more time creating useful software and less time bogged down with other activities.

The Compounding Cost of Sustainability Erosion

We notice a recurring pattern that often occurs in organizations that separate their workers. Code begins with a simple and easily maintainable structure. Over time, however, its complexity and instability increase in direct proportion to its declining quality. Here is a list of the code problems we often see.

- Unnecessarily complicated
- Over- or under-engineered

- Poorly performing
- Difficult and dangerous to modify

We believe this complexity problem is common. Many of us have experience with code that everyone is afraid to touch. We hear remarks like, "Don't touch that thing. It will break if you breathe on it."

We often have seen that code quality degrades over time, such that changing it becomes risky and expensive. We have accidentally accrued complexity that overwhelms our ability to master it when this happens. At that point, the development team typically throws up their hands and exclaims, "We need to re-architect this!"

Many terms partially describe this process of steadily increasing complexity, but we want a standard. Let's walk through these terms before defining our own.

A common term we hear is Technical Debt [8], but we believe this word has come to mean more than its original definition.

As originally defined, Technical Debt describes purposefully deploying software to Production when we don't yet fully understand the problem domain so that we can gain a better understanding. Once we gain an understanding, we go back and update our code, so it reflects our updated knowledge. If we fail to update our code, the debt eventually accrues enough interest that we can no longer make forward progress.

Technical Debt partly describes the pattern we observe, but it isn't quite the same. We often see overly complicated and unstable code that people call Technical Debt. Such code doesn't meet the term's original definition because it's poor-quality software, not code that reflects an inadequate understanding of the problem domain.

Two terms that almost describe our observation are Accidental and Essential Complexity [9]. Accidental Complexity defines the complexity that we introduce in solving complex problems. This type of complexity can often be reduced. In contrast, Essential Complexity describes the inherent complexity of the problem space. It can't be made simpler.

While close, Accidental and Essential Complexity are distinct from the type of over-complication and instability we see.

Software Entropy [10] is another term that closely, but not precisely, describes our observations. The term describes the pattern of software essentially rotting over time. Modifications to a running system inevitably increase its complexity. And with time, changes in the software's operating environment eventually render its technology obsolete. Entropy describes much of what we see, but in our view, it doesn't wholly capture the over-complication and instability.

Cruft is another term that partially describes what we see. Cruft is defined as the build-up of unused or leftover code and internal deficiencies that add complexity [11]. This cruft causes a steady increase in the difficulty of modifying the software. This term nearly describes what we have seen, but we believe the problem extends beyond just cruft.

When complexity and instability overwhelm us, we often fall into the Capability Trap [12]. We're so pressured to meet deadlines and our code so difficult to modify that workers are forced into overtime to keep the system running and hopefully push out new features.

Once we begin working overtime, our time to improve the system is reduced, and we steadily erode our capability to release new software and improve the code. This reduced capability leads to even more overtime and more pressure in a vicious circle, leaving even less time for improvements.

Unfortunately, it's difficult to recognize that we have fallen into the Capability Trap. Research [12] indicates that this lack of recognition often stems from the long lead time between cause and effect, making it hard for us to see the connection and, therefore, more likely to attribute it to something else. Think of the long lead time between writing poor code and our awareness of its effect on the system, especially when working in silos that make us ignorant of each other's problematic code. As a result, we often can't correlate the two, meaning we will probably continue the flawed process.

We believe that we have observed a combination of all the above concepts that are magnified when we separate workers. We find that the growth of complexity and instability tends to follow a steadily-increasing pattern that mimics an exponential trend. This pattern causes the problems to compound with time, eventually hindering our ability to update and maintain the software.

At this point, the inevitable demands begin for a complete software rewrite, and we hear the statement, "We need to re-architect this!" Unfortunately, if workers are still separated, the cycle often restarts with the new version of the code. Then, sometime in the future, the team will again throw up its hands and demand a re-architecture.

We call this process of steadily increasing complexity ***Sustainability Erosion***. Our ability to maintain our code and control its complexity steadily erodes with time. It can't be sustained because the code becomes too complex, bug-ridden, and fragile to update.

> *We call this process of steadily increasing complexity Sustainability Erosion.*

We believe that Sustainability Erosion is more likely to occur when we separate our workers. When separated, it's harder to promote practices that keep our code clean and simple such as code reviews, design reviews, and Test-Driven Development. It's also harder to spot recurring code patterns that should be refactored into reusable modules because there's no shared memory of the entire codebase.

By contrast, everyone shares a common memory of the code and a joint responsibility to maintain its quality when working together. These common factors make it more likely to produce better quality work, helping us avoid creating the complexity that eventually overwhelms us. That's not to say that Software Teaming will always guarantee that we never experience Sustainability Erosion. But it's been our experience that it's profoundly reduced.

So, "Won't This Cost Too Much?"

Now we can finally answer the question, "Is Software Teaming Cost-Effective?" We believe it has been for us due to the savings we achieve when we reduce the hidden costs of separating workers. But that's only for us.

We want to be clear. We're speaking only for our experience and no one else's. We can't definitively prove that Software Teaming is cost-effective. Nor can we prove that it isn't. We certainly aren't saying that you will discover cost savings if you try Software Teaming. We simply don't know.

On the other hand, we also can't prove that the default state of separating workers is cost-effective. We have our doubts. We wonder how often its cost-effectiveness is demonstrated before people implement it.

In short, it comes down to our opinion. We base it on the results we've seen in our work environments only. Your opinion and experiences may differ.

We don't know what's cost-effective for others. We believe everyone must decide for themselves.

References

1. Williams, Laurie and Erdogmus, Hakan. On the Economic Feasibility of Pair Programming. International Workshop on Economics-Driven Software Engineering in conjunction with the International Conference on Software Engineering, May 2002.

2. Jones, Capers. Software Quality Metrics: Three Harmful Metrics and Two Helpful Metrics. Namcook Analytics, LLC. June 6, 2012.

3. Gross, N., M. Stepanek, O. Port, and J. Carey. "Software Hell," in Business Week, 1999, pp. 104-118, 1999.

4. Rico, Dr. David F., Sayani, Dr. Hasan H., Sone, Dr. Saya. J. The Business Value of Agile Software Methods, Maximizing ROI with Just-In-Time Processes and Documentation. Ross Publishing, 2009.

5. Hannay, Jo E., Dyba, Tore, Arisholm, Erik, Sjoberg, Dag I. K. The Effectiveness of Pair Programming: A Meta-Analysis. Information and Software Technology. Vol 51(7). July 2009.

6. Arisholm, E., Gallis, H., Dyba, T., Sjoberg, D.I.K. Evaluating Pair Programming with Respect to System Complexity and Programmer Expertise. IEEE Transactions on Software Engineering, Vol. 33, Issue 2. 2007.

7. Vanhanen, J. and Lassenius, C. Effects of Pair Programming at the Development Team Level: an Experiment. International Symposium on Empirical Software Engineering. pp 336-345. 2005.

8. Ward Explains Debt Metaphor
   http://wiki.c2.com/?WardExplainsDebtMetaphor

9. Brooks, Fred. No Silver Bullet — Essence and Accident in Software Engineering. Proceedings of the IFIP Tenth World Computing Conference: 1069–1076.

10. Wasserman, A.Software Entropy Explained: Causes, Effects, and Remedies.

    https://www.toptal.com/software/software-entropy-explained

11. Fowler, Martin. Technical Debt.

    https://martinfowler.com/bliki/TechnicalDebt.html

12. Landry, E. and Sterman, J. The Capability Trap: Prevalence in Human Systems. In 35th International Conference of the System Dynamics Society (pp. 963-1010), July 2017.

10   Remote Software Teaming

Illustration © 2015 · Andrea Zuill

Introduction

Does everyone have to be in the same room to do Software Teaming? We don't think so.

When we first started Software Teaming, the group was co-located. We all worked in the same physical office, which made it easy to get together. We sat at the same table with one computer, a few keyboards, and projectors. We had whiteboards for discussing and diagramming our ideas, and we could move freely to the keyboard to write code. Conversations were simple and natural, and ideas moved from inception to code in a smooth flow.

Early on, one of our team members needed to work from home for a few months. We wanted to find a way they could work remotely as a fully engaged team member. There were obstacles to overcome, but we felt it was a worthwhile effort. That was the beginning of our exploration of remote Software Teaming. Since then, many other teams have found ways to make this work.

While it might be simpler for the whole team to work in the same physical space, the modern work environment often requires that people work from many different locations. Clearly, it's worthwhile to find a way to get Software Teaming's benefits while working remotely. Let's take a look at the possibilities and potential problems.

Advantages of Working Remotely

It's important to note that there are many benefits to working remotely. Indeed, there are enough benefits that we're well served by finding ways to do Software Teaming with remote team members. Here are just a few of the possible advantages:

- Our team is made up of the right people, regardless of their location.
- Finding great people is easier if they have flexible work arrangements and can work from any geographic location.
- There may be no need for a physical space if everyone can work out of their home.
- Putting together a team and working on the software might be quicker if no one needs to relocate.
- Flexibility for people with families: a baby at home, an elderly parent needing care, or simply personal preference.
- Some people are more comfortable if they can work from home instead of being in the same physical space as others.

"Turn Up The Good" on Working Remotely

Working remotely doesn't have to mean working independently. Instead, we can Turn Up The Good on working remotely. The same good things we get from Software Teaming when co-located apply when remote. These things include continuous design and code review, all the people needed for decision-making on hand and in the same context, and each contributing their best effort when it's most needed. These items are just as meaningful regardless of how we work.

How do We do This?

When working remotely, the main concerns are having an environment that allows us to collaborate and a protocol that makes communication easy.

With modern conferencing tools, we can set up a virtual space comparable in many aspects to a physical workspace. It can be very close to physically working side-by-side and face-to-face.

There are many choices for setting up remote conferencing, and the technology changes so quickly that we can't make recommendations. At a high level, you'll need the following items.

- Video collaboration so everyone's face is visible, and we can talk to each other.
- Screen sharing capability where the code is visible to everyone.
- Keyboard sharing so everyone can act as the Driver when needed.
- Whiteboarding so everyone can write ideas, giving us a shared space for exchanging thoughts and deriving solutions.

We also need a protocol for how we interact: whose turn it is to talk, rotating at the keyboard, and when to pause for discussion. A protocol ensures that conversation flows seamlessly and the Driver-Navigator pattern is easy to use.

Are We Effective When We're Remote?

Does remote Software Teaming work as well as when we're co-located? We're not sure this is a meaningful question. Perhaps a more meaningful question is: can we improve our results with Software Teaming if we're working remotely?

We've done a substantial amount of remote Software Teaming over the years and found it highly effective. We believe that we can effectively work together, whether co-located or remote.

Things are Different When We're Remote

While the basic principles of Software Teaming are the same whether we're remote or co-located, there are some differences to consider when working remotely. A list of some significant differences and ideas on handling them follows.

Conversation Protocol

Getting good at remote conversations is essential because they can be more difficult than when co-located. For example, when we're co-located, it's easy to determine who has the speaker's right-of-way by using normal social cues. Conversations must be managed differently when remote because the cues aren't as obvious.

We need a means of avoiding interrupting each other and allowing each person to share their ideas. We can manage this with protocols, tooling, and manners. Here are some suggested protocols for better communication.

- Use the meeting tool "raised hand" icon to indicate we have something to contribute.
- Use colored index cards. Each color has a specific meaning. For example, a red card means you have an urgent contribution. A yellow card means you have something to contribute, but it can wait.
- Prefer action over endless debate. We try it as soon as we have an idea instead of continuing to debate it.
- Use a virtual whiteboard as a shared space for capturing conversations. We cover this in more detail below.

Virtual Meeting Software

When physically sitting together, it's easy to see and speak with each other, making it simple to stay engaged in conversations. When remote, teams must find a way to communicate that gives them a similar level of effectiveness.

We use virtual meeting software for team communication (examples include Zoom© and Google Meet©). This software uses video and audio to approximate physically sitting together at a workstation. It allows us to see and hear each other, making staying engaged as a team easier even though we're remote. Using high-quality cameras and microphones improves the experience.

We've found it's much easier to have engaged conversations when we can see each other's faces. It may not be possible to do this in all environments. For instance, some people may prefer to leave their cameras off. Also, slow internet connections can limit video use.

We suggest experimenting with ways to make video use natural, sustainable, and comfortable. For example, it's helpful to take frequent breaks, either individually or as a team. The team can also try turning the cameras off occasionally.

Development Environment Types

Teams typically gather around a physical development environment displayed on large monitors when co-located. With this arrangement, it's easy for everyone to see the code. It's also easy to switch Drivers because the new Driver simply rolls their chair up to the keyboard.

It's trickier to arrange this when remote, but it can be done. Below, we list some remote arrangements of development environments.

Server-Based Development Environment

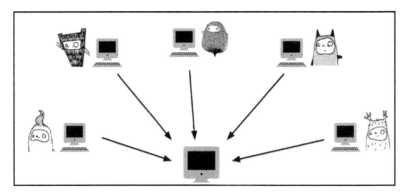

Example of Server-Based Development Environment

With this arrangement, we have a development environment on a remote server that's functionally equivalent to the team workstation we would use when co-located. It's a high-powered computer with fast network connections and all the tools and access to services we need for building software. Typically, it's located on the organization's network, giving it access to code repositories, databases, spreadsheets, browsers, email, and anything else we require, but it can also be in the cloud.

We suggest making the server computer a standalone computer used only for remoting purposes so other tasks don't slow it. We recommend that you keep it up to date with the latest iteration of fast CPU, hard-drives, and network hardware.

Instead of being physically present in front of a team computer, as we would when co-located, each team member uses remote desktop software to provide access to the server computer. Each team member logs into the remote server and views it on their local screen. With proper access, they can work as if they were physically sitting at the remote computer.

There are many remote desktop software applications, and we recommend experimenting with them to choose which best suits the team's needs (examples include AnyDesk© and TeamViewer©). We also suggest that you use one application as your primary remoting software while maintaining a second as a backup. If the primary software is unavailable, you can fall back on the second and keep the team working.

We suggest using the video and audio from your virtual meeting software, even if your remote desktop software has those capabilities. Using the virtual meeting software's capabilities creates a better experience for everyone.

When rotating Drivers, the new Driver takes control of the desktop, and the previous Driver relinquishes it. We find it helpful to disable keyboard and mouse access when it isn't your turn to drive. This technique prevents accidentally taking control of the remote environment. As with co-location, there's no need to check in or retrieve the latest code when changing Drivers.

One benefit of a Server-Based Development Environment is that switching Drivers is a simple and quick task. The new Driver simply takes control of the remote machine, and the work continues, minimizing interruption to the team's flow.

Another benefit is that adding new team members requires only the addition of new login accounts. There's no need to configure a new workstation for each new team member.

An additional benefit is that remote desktop software is usually cross-platform. Each team member can connect to the remote server regardless of their local operating system. Also, any lag in the remote server will be experienced almost equally by each team member, thus minimizing the likelihood that some team members will be disadvantaged.

A final benefit is that only the remote server must be a high-powered machine. Such a machine is optional for each team member.

For these reasons, we prefer the Server-Based Development Environment over the others discussed below.

Multiple Individual Developer Environments

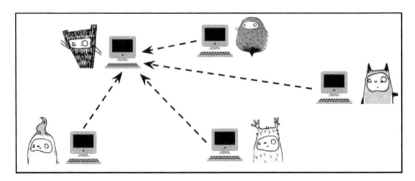

Example of Multiple Individual Developer Environments

With this setup, each team member has a workstation functionally equivalent to the team workstation we would use when co-located. Each workstation has access to the tools, code repository, and other artifacts required to build the software and complete the team's other work. During a Software Teaming session, each Driver uses the virtual meeting software to share their local screen when it's their turn to drive.

With this arrangement, we create a temporary session branch when we start a new Software Teaming session [1]. Each Driver accesses the code on that branch, bringing it to their workstation instead of working at the server containing the code. The temporary branch is merged back into its parent when the work is completed [1].

When a Driver starts their turn, they share their screen, retrieve the current version of the code from the temporary branch, and start coding as directed by the Navigators. When the Driver finishes their turn, they push their changes to the temporary session branch regardless of the code's state, even if the tests aren't passing or the code isn't compiling. The next Driver repeats the steps by sharing their screen and retrieving the code.

With each Driver, we repeat the steps above until we're ready to merge the code into its parent branch.

A significant benefit of Multiple Individual Developer Environments is the minimal effort required to set it up. If everyone on the team is already working remotely, connecting them for Software Teaming requires only virtual meeting software, which they're probably already using.

One Individual Developer Environment

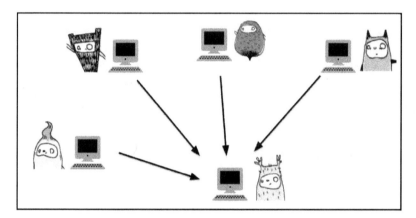

Example of One Individual Developer Environment

This arrangement allows a team member's computer to become the Software-Teaming session's host workstation. One team member uses the virtual meeting software's remote control feature to share their workstation's keyboard, screen, and mouse. This workstation has access to the tools, code repository, and other artifacts required to build the software and complete the team's other work. If desired, the team can switch to another member's computer and use it as the host workstation at any time.

At the start of the session, a team member shares their computer screen with the rest of the team. This host workstation will be where everyone works for the duration of the Software Teaming session.

When a Driver starts their turn, they take control of the workstation and begin coding at the direction of the Navigators. When switching Drivers, the new Driver simply takes control of the host workstation.

One issue with this approach is that shortcut keys may not work as expected. Additionally, the shared computer is unusable by its owner without disrupting the Driver. There may also be problems with keyboard lag. We discuss keyboard lag in detail in the Internet Connection Throughput section below.

We recommend experimenting with different brands of virtual meeting software to see which is best for your use.

As with Multiple Individual Developer Environments, a benefit of One Individual Developer Environment is that everyone already has their own computer and access to the team's code if they're working remotely. Connecting everyone requires only virtual meeting software.

Cloud-Based Development Environment

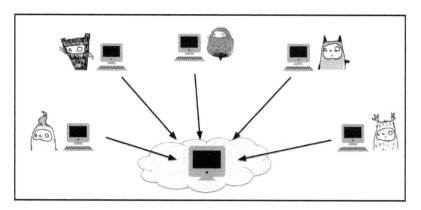

Example of Cloud-Based Development Environment

One environment that shows excellent potential is the cloud-based environment. Each environment we've described above requires building a development environment from scratch. By contrast, cloud-based environments are already created, and using them requires only configuring them for your desired aims. Our experience with them is limited, but we see some benefits:

- They require only a browser.
- Everyone gets the same configuration instead of having to set up their own locally and contend with differences between each others' setups.
- They include a wide variety of programming languages from which to choose.
- They integrate with the provider's other cloud services.

These are powerful platforms. Given that features in these environments are rapidly evolving, we think it won't be long before they're a viable choice for some teams.

Screens

We suggest using at least two high-quality, large monitors in your local environment. We find that having multiple large monitors makes it easier to do the work. We like to place the Software Teaming workstation on one monitor and the virtual meeting window on the other.

When remotely controlling a host's computer, the host can accidentally take back control when doing work-related side tasks. This problem results from two people having control of one computer. Using two monitors lessens the likelihood of this happening.

Whiteboards

We use whiteboards as the place where we organize the flow of our work and think together as a team when we're co-located. This collaboration is more difficult when we're remote, but there are software tools that allow us to approximate it.

We use a combination of software programs to simulate in-person whiteboards. We use shared cloud documents for writing text, allowing everyone to view and edit as a team. For actual whiteboards, we use virtual whiteboard software that allows everyone to see and contribute to the work. These virtual whiteboards include features like sticky notes, voting, grids, and other items that simulate physical whiteboards.

Virtual whiteboards are difficult because you can't pick up a pen and draw as you would on a physical whiteboard. However, by using a tablet and stylus device, you can draw or write almost as easily as if you were at a physical whiteboard. When the drawing is shared with the team, anything someone adds is visible to everyone in real-time, mimicking a physical whiteboard.

While these tools aren't as effective as in-person whiteboards, they still allow us to collaborate when remote and are much better than attempting to do so without them. Whiteboard software is quickly evolving, and the usability gap between physical and virtual whiteboards is steadily reducing.

Using a Timer

When co-located, a timer can be as simple as someone's phone sitting on a table. A timer is trickier when remote. If using a phone, the team may not hear it in someone's local environment, especially if that person is muted.

Online versions of Software Teaming timers include Driver and Navigator roles, automatic rotations, and adding and removing team members by name. They allow everyone to see and share the timer software, keeping the team in sync. These online timers are more effective than using someone's phone, and we prefer them.

Time Zones

Time zones are simple when a Software Teaming group is co-located because everyone is in the same physical space and time zone. When remote, however, teams may have members in different time zones.

It might be difficult if more than a few hours separate team member time zones. Consider setting aside scheduled time blocks that are the best compromise for everyone involved. We suggest experimenting to see what works well for your situation. Even if time zones prevent us from working together all day, we've found even a few hours together is still helpful.

Internet Connection Throughput

Internet connection throughput is the data transfer rate per unit of time for an individual's internet connection. Throughput isn't a concern when a Software Teaming group is co-located because their office's connection speed is usually quite fast. However, when team members are remote, throughput is sometimes limited, significantly limiting collaboration.

Limited-throughput environments can be unusable when using a keyboard, audio, and video simultaneously. Turning off your camera's video feed usually helps, speeding up everything else.

If throughput is low for one or more team members, keyboard sharing may introduce time lags between action and result. If these lags are problematic, whoever has the fastest connection can work as the Driver for the entire session with everyone else navigating.

Whenever possible, we suggest obtaining the fastest connection available to improve collaboration.

Taking Frequent Breaks

We find that it's sometimes more tiring to be in a remote video meeting than co-located with a Software Teaming group. We aren't sure why, but we suspect it has something to do with having a camera pointed at you all day and the physical restrictions that result.

When co-located, we're free to move about, especially when regularly changing Drivers. Additionally, there isn't a camera pointed at us. Instead, the team focuses on the code in front of them.

When remote, we must remain in camera and audio range so our teammates can see and talk with us. For some of us, this is tiring and requires that we take more frequent breaks than we would when co-located. If you're taking a break by going for a walk, you can stay in the virtual meeting by bringing your phone with you.

Shared Problems

When working as a co-located Software Teaming group, all problems are dealt with as team problems to be solved by the team. The same applies when working remotely.

When a remote member has trouble with their development environment or other issues, it's essential to realize this is a team problem, and the team can solve it together. Working together on the problem improves everyone's understanding by spreading knowledge among the group. We have found that it also leads to a sense of team cohesion.

Hybrid Software Teaming

Hybrid Software Teaming is an advanced technique that includes co-located and remote team members in the same session. It requires far more skill and consideration than being entirely co-located or remote. If you decide to try this, we suggest you work diligently to ensure that remote team members are fully engaged with the rest of the team.

One significant drawback of the hybrid approach is that the co-located and remote team members don't share the same experience. The co-located team members can easily converse with each other, but communication is more difficult for remote members.

Often the co-located members share one microphone and camera for the whole team. As a result, the remote members don't see individual faces on their monitor, making it difficult to know who is talking at any given moment.

Another issue is that when sharing the co-located screen, everyone onsite can see the shared screen and any other screens the team is using. The remote team members might only see the primary shared screen, making it harder for them to grasp the context.

One way to partially offset communication problems is to place separate computers, such as laptops, at eye level to display each remote person's face individually in the co-located environment. Doing this makes conversing with them more natural.

Another way to equalize the experience between co-located and remote team members is for each co-located member to sit in their own space as if they were fully remote. This technique sidesteps the challenges of the hybrid approach and is our preferred method when we have both co-located and remote team members.

Switching from Co-located to Remote

Here's an idea if you're currently working co-located but need to change to working remotely. You can experiment with a simulated "remote" team by setting up separate work areas for each team member in the same physical office. You can then practice screen and keyboard sharing as if you were remotely located. When problems arise, you can quickly gather to troubleshoot the setup.

Once the remote spaces are set up, you can practice communicating, navigating, coding, and anything else you need to resolve. As you build confidence in working this way, you can move on by adding truly remote team members one at a time as everyone gains experience and becomes comfortable working remotely. Alternatively, everyone can switch to remote at the same time.

Exploring and Experimenting

We can't provide a simple recipe for how remote Software Teaming will work for you. We suggest continuous experimenting, inspecting, and adapting to help steer toward an effective environment that works for your particular situation.

Other Resources

For greater detail on remote Software Teaming, see the website RemoteMobProgramming.org or the book of the same name [1]. We've found them to be excellent sources of information.

References

1. Christ, Jochen. Harrer, Simon. Huber, Martin. Remote Mob Programming. LeanPub. 2020.

Part Four: Teams

Illustration © 2013 - Andrea Zuill

This section discusses the nature of teams in software engineering and how they're usually structured. We contrast the typical structure with our alternative of a Software Teaming group. We also discuss the skills and qualities needed for proper teamwork. When you finish this section, you should understand how to work well in a Software Teaming group.

1   The Reality of Teams

Illustration © 2014 - Andrea Zuill

Teams are one of the most heavily-promoted concepts in most organizations. Think of the countless posters listing the benefits of teamwork, team-building exercises, and statements to "be a team player" or "take one for the team." Teams are something that we value highly in our world. Yet, as we will see below, our actions don't often live up to our words.

Why a Team?

What's the purpose of teams, and why do we need them? We need teams because we want to accomplish work that one person can't accomplish independently. Usually, the tasks require various cross-cutting skills that one person rarely possesses, so we recruit talent from a pool that encompasses all the skills necessary.

We also require teams if one person has the skills and knowledge, but there's far too much work for that person to handle. Indeed, if we found one person with all the requisite capabilities and there was no rush to complete the work, then we would only need to clear that person's schedule, assign them the job, and let them proceed. There would be no need for a team. For small and straightforward work, this is what we do. We simply give the task to one person. But this isn't the case for large, complex tasks, so we must assemble a team to accomplish the work.

Two Types of Teams

There are a variety of team structures, but we're interested in two of the most common types: the functional team and the cross-functional team.

A functional team focuses on one type of work. Examples include a requirements team, a development team, or a testing team. We group the people because they share common expertise. They work on features or stories associated with their expertise and typically operate separately from the other team members. The work is coordinated via meetings, documents, emails, phone calls, and other periodic integration points.

By contrast, a cross-functional team brings together people of different functional expertise. For example, a team might consist of product experts, designers, programmers, and testers. They work together on the same feature or set of stories. We hope to get many possible benefits from working this way.

- Team members can help each other whenever needed.
- Communication barriers are minimized as everyone has easy access and communicates frequently.
- Because work is completed in "small bits," we get rapid feedback and use it to make decisions as a group.

A Team in Name Only

Many of us work on a "team in name only" in software development. We work individually, gather for meetings, and periodically merge our work and ideas. Is this really teamwork? We don't think so.

Simply bringing people together to work on something doesn't necessarily create a team. Almost everybody in software development is on a "team," but they do almost nothing we recognize as teamwork.

Why would we work individually and come together only for meetings if we're on a team? Few teams outside of software engineering work like this and still call themselves a team. What about members of an orchestra giving a concert? Do they play independently? No, they all work together on the same thing, at the same time, in the same place.

Orchestras are structured deliberately to optimize the flow of the music, not the busyness of the individual musicians. There are long periods when some musicians don't play their instruments, but they're instantly available when needed.

This approach means that some slack is built into the system. Everyone accepts that this is necessary for satisfactory performance. The slack is an insurance policy: we're willing to pay the salary for someone who isn't always needed because of the cost to us when that person is necessary and unavailable. This might seem wasteful, but it's far more wasteful for an entire team to stop work and wait for the required person.

We could learn a thing or two from orchestras.

In the software world, why do we so often separate team members? We think it stems from the misguided notion that we get more things done when we work independently. In the case of a team with five members, we believe that we get five things done at once if everyone is working separately. This is only true if all of the following conditions are also true. (For more details on this, see the chapter Won't This Cost Too Much?)

- There must be no dependencies between team members. Thus no one ever waits on someone else to finish so they can start.
- Each team member must have all the required knowledge to perform their work. They must never interrupt each other's work by asking for help, which causes costly context-switching.
- Meetings are never required to ensure that everyone is aligned.

- No one accidentally codes a bug because their work isn't being inspected.
- No one ever needs to merge their code with that of others.
- There's no need to do integration testing of the separate pieces after merging.

Obviously, this list of conditions is never true in software engineering. So why do we structure our teams like we do?

One reason is that it's thought to be easier to manage.

Often, the typical team is optimized for ease of management instead of the team's effectiveness, making it easy for managers at the team's expense. Instead, we should be making it easy to get the work done.

Here is the crucial question: what if we allow people to work together to solve problems as a team instead of separating them? That's what we'll discuss next.

2   The Team, the Whole Team, and Nothing but the Team

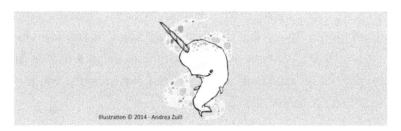

Illustration © 2014 · Andrea Zuill

In contrast to a team of separated individuals, a Software Teaming group is one where everyone works together. We define a team as a group of individuals with a common purpose who help each other do the work. They benefit from continuous communication and integrate their ideas in "real-time" as a group. In other words, they work together, literally.

Whole Team Together

In Extreme Programming, one of the practices is "Whole Team Together." For us, a well-formed Whole Team will be made up of everyone who contributes to the work at hand. When we have all the required knowledge and skills on the team, each work item flows from start to finish without being blocked. If questions arise, someone on the team can answer them. We have everyone we need to do the work.

We're often asked, "How many people should be on the team?". The answer is *however many it takes to get the work done*. An effective Software Teaming group might include testers, developers, designers, database experts, product owners, and anyone else needed to accomplish the job. When there's missing knowledge or capability, the work slows down or becomes blocked as we try to get the knowledge or find someone to help.

The team is best equipped to determine who is needed on the team. When we find ourselves frequently blocked waiting on knowledge or skills we don't have, it's a sign we might need to add a team member. Alternatively, we can fill a gap by learning the skill or gaining the knowledge ourselves.

If the need for this knowledge is infrequent, it might be sufficient to find someone to work with the team for a short time to unblock us. We find it helpful to pay close attention to this because frequently waiting for temporary help destroys the flow of the work.

Ideally, every team member remains in the work context by working together. We grow a shared understanding, so making decisions and steering the work occurs smoothly, without interruption or blocking. We don't spend time bringing someone up to speed whenever we have a question or need help.

3   The Qualities of a Software Teaming Group

Illustration © 2013 - Andrea Zuill

Working Well Together

Software Teaming is focused on finding ways to work well together so we can achieve continuous collaboration. Here are some of the qualities we see when we collaborate.

- Everyone works together to solve a problem instead of simultaneously working on different issues.
- We accentuate the idea that we're here to help each other.
- Each team member is looking for ways to contribute the right thing at the right time and in the right way.
- We benefit from various skills, skill levels, personality types, backgrounds, perspectives, and experiences.
- We're open to serendipity, innovation, sharing ideas, and trying new things.
- To limit "group think," we constantly challenge and scrutinize our decisions.
- We encourage differences of opinion without conflicts of personality.
- We have a bias towards action rather than argument.

- There's no "ownership" of ideas. We freely share them and don't expect them to be separated from the team's ideas. We accept that they'll grow and change as we move toward a solution.
- The focus is to work together to find a solution instead of "getting MY work done."

These qualities provide us with significant benefits. Chief among them is that we maximize the amount of high-quality, useful software. That's a goal well worth striving toward.

We maximize the amount of high-quality, useful software.

---

4   Personal Skills Needed for Teamwork

Illustration © 2012 - Andrea Zuill

Many of us spend our programming careers working independently. Think of all the time we work alone, lost in our thoughts, coding away as we solve problems, coming up for air only when strictly necessary. With this kind of experience, it's natural to wonder if we have the interpersonal skills to work with others in a Software Teaming group.

The good news is that we believe all of us have the skills or can learn them, and we simply need to know what's expected of us when we join a team. We also believe that teamwork is something we bring to the group, not something we get from it.

In no particular order, the skills we feel are most necessary are listed below. Don't fret if you think that you lack one or more skills. Our experience is that everyone can learn them with practice and help from supportive teammates. They will soon become second nature with time, even if they seem alien on our first try.

Intellectual Humility

Being intellectually humble is crucial to being an effective team member. We must accept that we don't know everything and that no one can. This makes it easy to acknowledge that other peoples' ideas might be better than ours.

In some ways, being intellectually humble is a great stress reliever because we're freed of the burden of proving to ourselves and others that we're smart and capable. Ironically, this cognitive ease might mean we're more likely to find innovative ways to solve problems. We think this innovation often escapes us when we're rigidly focused on proving our intellectual worth.

Intellectual humility also means we're willing to admit being wrong, which is probably most of the time, and we don't know it yet. Because being wrong and not knowing it feels just like being right [1]. Indeed, being right and being wrong are indistinguishable until the moment we're proven wrong. That alone vouches for the idea of being intellectually humble.

If you're a senior developer, being intellectually humble means being willing to seek and try junior developers' ideas. It's surprising how often those ideas turn out to be both innovative and effective. And nothing boosts the confidence of a junior developer quicker than having the senior developer try their ideas, especially when paired with a compliment.

Intellectual humility also means we abandon an idea when it isn't working and try something else instead of being trapped in the Sunk Cost Fallacy. (Briefly, the Sunk Cost Fallacy means that time and money already spent can't be recovered, but we're unwilling to see that and spend more of both seeking a return on our initial outlay.) Intellectually humble developers don't waste time trying to prove they're right when something fails. They let go of it and move on.

Being intellectually humble means that we're willing to allow others to get the credit. We're happy to see the success of others when we surrender the need to display our cognitive skills. It also means that we willingly listen to the ideas of others and experiment with them, even when—or especially when—we disagree or think they won't succeed.

A story from Kevin: Some time ago, I was a patient undergoing a medical test. The attending physician was an experienced doctor with a flock of young interns following him on his rounds and hanging on his every word, eagerly absorbing his wisdom.

He examined and diagnosed me as he awaited the results of a test he had ordered. When the test results contradicted his diagnosis, he immediately turned to the interns and said, "OK, I was wrong."

I was struck by how quickly and easily he said the words. There was no hesitation, excuse-making, rationalization, or anything of the sort. He never attempted to minimize his error by saying something like, "It's an easy mistake to make. Anyone else would have said the same thing."

He embodied intellectual humility and showed no sunk costs in his first diagnosis. I don't know if the young interns realized it or not, but they had just witnessed something more valuable than medical knowledge: the humility to admit error and change course.

Empathy

A well-developed sense of empathy is helpful for a Software Teaming group member. An empathetic team member quietly sits when others speak, patiently waiting for their turn. They listen carefully for the quiet voices who may fear expressing their thoughts and find gentle ways to let them share.

An empathetic team member tries to act with Kindness, Consideration, and Respect. They also apologize when they step on someone's toes and resist defending their behavior when it has strayed. Finally, exhibiting empathy means committing to the ease of others so that every team member feels safe expressing their ideas.

These abilities aren't always natural or easy. But as with other Software Teaming skills, they can be learned, especially when we're willing to make ourselves vulnerable enough to ask for our teammates' help in learning them.

References

1. "On Being Wrong" by Kathyrn Schulz.
    https://www.ted.com/talks/kathryn_schulz_on_being_wrong?language=en

Part Five: The Power of Flow

Illustration © 2013 - Andrea Zuill

This part of the book describes the power of flow achieved with Software Teaming. We address how a group of programmers could be more effective than individuals working alone. We attribute this effectiveness to flow.

When you finish this section, you should understand the benefits of flow that will help you decide if you want to pursue Software Teaming in your environment.

1   The Productivity Question

Illustration © 2013 · Andrea Zuill

How Can Five People At One Computer Be Productive?

We're often asked this question: How can five people at one computer be productive? We answered this from a cost perspective in the chapter Won't This Cost Too Much?, but here, we want to address the idea of productivity versus effectiveness.

Initially, while we knew Software Teaming was very productive for us, we didn't understand what was driving it. We saw how much waste disappeared simply because many of our problems faded away when working together as a team (see Part Six for details).

Our product owners and customers were getting useful software sooner and more frequently. Our manager had fewer problems to deal with. Our work quality was very high, and everyone on the team, our manager, and our customers were thrilled with the results.

We transformed from a struggling team to a shining team. These benefits got us wondering about a way to understand how it happened.

Changing the Question

We might better answer the productivity question with a different sort of question. Peter Block puts it this way:

"Transformation comes more from pursuing profound questions than seeking practical answers."

Peter Block

It's worth considering this: the answer isn't as important as having the right question. Pondering a good question reveals an even better question, and eventually, we find a question that almost resolves itself.

In our view, productivity isn't as meaningful as effectiveness. There's often a focus on productivity without questioning if it's effective.

The overriding philosophy in many organizations is that we're wasting money if everyone isn't fully utilized at all times. The belief is that keeping everyone busy is productive because "we're getting a lot of things done." We often miss the bigger picture of being effective when we relentlessly focus only on keeping everyone fully tasked. For us, effectiveness is about focusing on better outcomes.

Here's a simple example: are we effective if we're one-hundred percent tasked with building software that no one will ever use? We could certainly state that we're productive. The problem is that we aren't being effective. It doesn't matter how much we produce if we're working on the wrong things. This sometimes happens when we focus only on productivity and neglect to consider effectiveness.

With Software Teaming, we aim primarily to be effective and concern ourselves less with productivity. It's a subtle shift in philosophy, but it profoundly affects our work. In our view, it's far better to ensure we're being effective by working on the right things.

With effectiveness in mind, let's reverse and rephrase the question into something we consider more meaningful.

> *How can we be effective if we separate the people who should be working together?*

The original productivity question implies that separating people is productive, and our new question suggests that gathering people is effective.

It would be wonderful if there were a reliable means of measuring effectiveness. To do so would require established metrics for measuring it, which don't exist. If effectiveness is what we want and can't directly measure it, let's seek insight by asking yet another question: *What are the things that destroy effectiveness?*

What Things Destroy Effectiveness?

To determine how we might be more effective, we can start by looking at what destroys effectiveness. Let's list some things that make work unnecessarily difficult and prevent us from getting good results. The following responses are taken from workshops and presentations when we ask, "What destroys effectiveness?"

- Context switching: working on something important and setting it aside to work on something else
- Bad code: meaningless names, long methods, deeply nested if statements
- Meetings
- The person we need to get an answer from isn't available
- Gold-plating, doing more than is needed

- Unclear or missing requirements
- No comments in the code
- Comments that are misleading or not relevant
- Too many comments in the code
- Emails
- Interruptions
- Dead code
- Noisy work area
- Quiet work area
- Working on too many things, multitasking
- Team members are taken off the team to work on other "important" things
- Bugs
- Wrong or missing unit tests
- Insufficient automated tests, such as unit tests and integration tests
- Needing to do status reports and other busywork
- Estimating
- Slow computers, inadequate equipment
- Difficulties getting access to the database, development environment, or requirements documents
- Surfing the web

The list is nearly endless. While there are many commonalities, there are also contradictions. What destroys effectiveness for one person may not be what destroys it for another. Each individual and organization will have its own list.

What We Found with Software Teaming

We didn't set out to solve these effectiveness problems. Many of them merely faded away, and this was a revelation.

Now we can answer the original question, "How can we be effective with five people working at a single computer?" *We no longer need to deal with problems that plague us when working separately.*

Here are a few examples

- We no longer wait for answers to questions because the people with the answers are sitting and working with us.
- With everyone reviewing the code continuously, the code is of much better quality.
- Things get done sooner when the whole team focuses on one thing at a time.
- We deliver functionality into actual use very quickly so its value can be proven or changed to meet the desired result.

These things are hard to do working separately, but less so when working together.

"The whole is greater than the sum of its parts."

Anonymous

We have noticed that when working as a Software Teaming group, the whole is greater than the sum of the parts.

The Sum of the Parts:

The Whole:

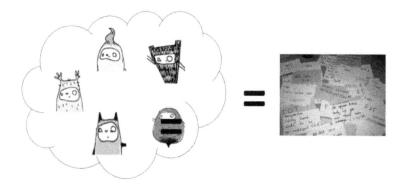

Another Way to Think About It

Perhaps this is something meaningful to consider: is it essential to get the most work out of each person? Or is it more important to get the best of everyone into everything we do?

> *Software Teaming is not about getting the most work out of each person. It is about getting the best of everyone into everything we do.*

How do we change our work approach if getting the best from everyone is one of our goals?

We changed how we work by using Software Teaming and found that we got the best of everyone into everything we do. A wonderful consequence is that we were much more effective.

2 Types of Flow

Illustration © 2013 · Andrea Zuill

Psychological Flow

Psychological Flow is an individual's ability to achieve a mental state that makes the work effortless and enjoyable. In programming, we often call this "being in the zone." It's an exalted state where the code seems almost to write itself, flowing effortlessly from our minds and into our computers. Time passes without notice, and everything around us falls away as our focus turns only to the code in front of us.

Psychologist Mihaly Csikszentmihalyi describes the flow state as follows[1].

"A state in which people are so involved in an activity that nothing else seems to matter; the experience is so enjoyable that people will continue to do it even at great cost, for the sheer sake of doing it."

Mihaly Csikszentmihalyi

Every programmer finds this state at some point and seeks to reach it again. Still, it's difficult to achieve because of barriers such as emails, phone calls, interruptions from coworkers, noisy office environments, meetings, and a limitless list of other distractions.

Given how desirable this flow state is, it seems like we would do everything possible to achieve it, which leads to an obvious question we always hear whenever someone first learns about Software Teaming.

"How can I achieve flow when I'm working with others?"

It's a sensible question. After all, flow is hard enough to achieve on our own, so how would we ever hope to achieve it if we're regularly in the company of others, with everyone trying to work together on the same computer at the same time? Isn't that just an impediment to the individual's ability to achieve flow?

Our guideline is that any team member is free to leave and work independently whenever they want, freeing them to pursue Psychological Flow as they see fit. We have found that team members will return to the team when they're ready, usually sharing what they have discovered, which benefits everyone.

The freedom to leave and rejoin means that no one feels that their creativity is constrained. We also find that members like staying on the team because they experience something they prefer: Team Flow, which we'll discuss next.

A story from Woody: One of the key lessons I take from trying to be Agile is "Turning Up the Good" (for more details, see Turn Up the Good). If we believe something is working well for us, what happens if we do more of it? If a little is good, then more might be better. This sort of test quickly tells us whether our "good" is indeed good or not.

Let's take the example of Turning Up the Good on working separately. Instead of placing workers in individual cubicles, how about if we put them in their own office, with a lockable door? How about if we move each person to a different city? How about if we move each person to opposite sides of the planet?

Another way of separating people is to put them out of phase with each other. I will work on the requirements in January. You will work on the design in February. Sally will work on the code in June. Mark will work on the testing in July.

If we try this, we will likely get a response like, "No, that's not what we mean. We want people to coordinate with each other." If that's the answer, let's turn up the good on coordination.

Team Flow

We discovered something interesting when we started working together as a Software Teaming group. Many problems plaguing an individual's ability to achieve Psychological Flow simply faded away (see Part Six for a detailed list of problems that faded away).

For example, we didn't have to attend meetings to provide status updates, disrupting our flow and taking time away from coding, when our status was on the computer screen in front of everyone. We weren't interrupted by coworkers seeking help when we were alongside each other doing the work together. There were no context-switching delays because we worked together on the same thing in the same context. There was no need to explain the same thing to different people at different times when everyone was present for the explanation. These delays and distractions were no longer a problem for us.

We found a surprising result: as a team, we got more work done and with higher quality than when we worked as individuals. We persistently achieved what appeared to be a flow state. Yet, it was different from what we knew as an individual's Psychological Flow, which each team member still achieved whenever they chose to work independently (working independently is an essential freedom for us). We were somehow also achieving flow as a team, a state that involves more than one person.

We unknowingly had stumbled upon Team Flow, which describes how teams achieve flow as a cohesive unit instead of as individuals. Jef van den Hout [2] identifies the following aspects of Team Flow.

- Collective ambition
- Common goal
- Aligned personal goals
- High skill integration
- Open communication
- Safety
- Mutual commitment
- Sense of unity
- Sense of joint progress
- Mutual trust
- Holistic focus

Our team included all the required skills and knowledge to solve problems. We didn't need to wait for answers or external expertise. There was a collective agreement to treat each other with Kindness, Consideration, and Respect so that everyone freely communicated their ideas without fear of ridicule or punishment. Individuals were no longer cognitively overloaded because they shared the workload, allowing members to contribute their best when they were best able. Together, these attributes led the team to achieve flow as a group.

There are many benefits to achieving Team Flow. Working as a group, we focus our cognitive power on a single work item instead of scattering our forces across the work landscape. This focus brings far more intellectual capacity to the problem, providing better-quality solutions, often more quickly. Additionally, when something blocks us, we don't need anyone's permission to investigate or escalate it. Instead, we simply tackle it.

We find that Team Flow is "collective flow." The team flows as a unit because there are sufficient people to maintain the focus at any point in time. There's less of the flow discontinuity seen when working individually because when working alone, there's no one to help us stay focused. In contrast, when working as a team, we help each other maintain focus and keep the flow going.

When the team reaches a flow state, the problems seem to solve themselves, and we know the best path forward to achieve solutions. Usually, the Team Flow is a dynamic state, with everyone sharing in the flow. The team moves forward as a group, with each person able to see the path ahead and what work needs to be done to get there.

We have noticed that if any team member drops out of the flow state, the rest maintain sufficient flow to continue. We find this more helpful than an individual's Psychological Flow. Significantly, it's also more continuous, meaning that we achieve that magical flow state more often than when working alone. This continuous flow provides a crucial benefit: the work keeps moving, carrying it along from start to finish with fewer interruptions and distractions experienced when working independently.

Team Flow also solves a problem we often see. If a manager discovers one person's flow is blocked, they can "live with it" by telling the person to "work on something else." But if a manager sees the flow of an entire team blocked, the manager is more likely to remove the blockage. The problem is that when we work separately, many people are usually blocked at any given time, but it isn't as visible as when a team is blocked.

Most challenges in modern software environments are too complex for an individual, so we assign them to teams. Paradoxically, we then separate the team members and ask them to solve the problems individually. To us, it seems that we should work together and, in so doing, try to achieve flow as a team. We aren't alone in our beliefs. Consider van den Hout's description of Team Flow [2].

"... if the work environment were organized in a way that allows employees to experience flow as they tackle shared challenges, it would most likely result in increased enjoyment, satisfaction, personal development and shared performance. People will perform better together and their experience with team flow will likely encourage them to tackle new and even greater shared challenges."

Jef van den Hout

Research shows that team performance improves when team members experience Team Flow, particularly when they operate with Kindness, Consideration, and Respect, allowing for constructive and supportive feedback [2]. Together, performance improvement and team safety can motivate teams to attempt more difficult challenges. In our view, that's a worthwhile goal and why we seek to achieve Team Flow in our work environments.

Lean Flow

Illustration © 2015 · Andrea Zuill

In addition to Psychological Flow and Team Flow, we also realized we were experiencing another type of flow. Our software proceeded from concept to customer use with minimal delay. We weren't getting blocked on something and then putting it aside while waiting on an answer, which creates inventory and causes context-switching.

There was no queuing while we waited for answers from someone else. We didn't hand off our software to other departments for testing, approval, or deployment, thereby avoiding the associated queues and inventory creation. All of our work items proceeded from start to finish in a smooth, uninterrupted flow.

We soon realized that we had again stumbled upon a type of flow. In this case, it was Lean Flow, a flow found in lean manufacturing [3]. In lean manufacturing, an item goes from raw material to a finished product as quickly as possible with the minimum number of steps, delays, and waste. Waste is anything customers view as not adding value and for which they're unwilling to pay.

Examples of manufacturing waste are: paying to store a finished product in inventory while it waits to be used, paying a worker to transport an item to a location where it's needed, or paying a worker to wait idly while a required item is delivered.

We realized we were accomplishing Lean Flow with our software because our user stories went from idea to customer use with little delay or interruption. Our Team Flow made this Lean Flow possible, something we could never have achieved working separately.

Inventory

In lean manufacturing, inventory is defined as anything worked on but not yet delivering value to customers. It can be unfinished material required to create products or completed products awaiting delivery. These items sit idly by, pending their use, and are readily visible.

In software engineering, inventory is essentially invisible but is usually abundant. In our view, inventory in software development includes code not yet delivered to customers. It's usually waiting for completion, testing, approval, other code, or deployment. If the code is written but not yet used, we classify it as inventory.

Defined this way, it's apparent how much code can be classified as inventory in many organizations. It's usually buried deep in a source control repository, making it much harder to see than in a factory where it piles up on the shop floor. It isn't just code, either. Backlogs of user stories qualify as inventory if they represent ideas waiting to be implemented. In our view, inventory is anything where thinking has occurred, but its output hasn't been delivered to customers.

One way inventory enters a queue is when an individual programmer is blocked, and their manager tells them to "work on something else" to keep them busy. We find that many organizations are unaware of this dynamic. When everyone is fully utilized, we often believe we're productive and think, "Look how much work we're turning out." In reality, we're really saying, "Look how much inventory we're creating."

It's helpful to ask ourselves how much inventory we have at any given moment. The answer may be surprisingly large.

Queues

A queue is a line of things awaiting their turn to exit and continue moving. In formal terms, queues have an arrival, queue (line), servicing process, and exit. Everyday examples include waiting in a traffic jam, waiting in line at a supermarket, and waiting in line at a ticket counter.

In software, one way queues are created is when something is worked on and then waits to be used. They also occur when work in progress is blocked and waits to be unblocked. This waiting is far more common than we might realize.

Some obvious examples include software waiting to be reviewed, tested, or deployed and user stories awaiting coding. Less obvious examples include code that awaits refactoring "when we have time," user stories requiring estimation before coding, product managers so overloaded they can't respond to questions, and innumerable managerial approval gates. Once we define queueing as any waiting process, we see how pervasive queues are in most organizations.

According to Reinertsen [3], queues are the hidden, most significant waste in product development.

"Invisible and unmanaged queues are the root cause of poor economic performance in Product Development."

Donald Reinertsen

Queues result in longer delivery times, increased risk, greater overhead, lower quality, and poor morale [3]. They also delay crucial feedback, meaning workers waste time and money pursuing fruitless paths before discovering a better course. Queues are the inevitable byproduct of managers ensuring everyone is always fully utilized, leaving no slack in the system to absorb work surges. When everyone is one hundred percent busy, any new task must wait until someone is free to work on it. (Thus, the joke, "What do you call a freeway that's one-hundred percent utilized? A parking lot.")

Let's examine some hypothetical work situations that involve queues. The illustration below shows a typical eight-hour day under different queuing conditions. For this example, we work for one hour, and then we're blocked. This block might be, for example, a question to be answered by a product manager, meetings to attend, testing results we require, or approvals from a manager.

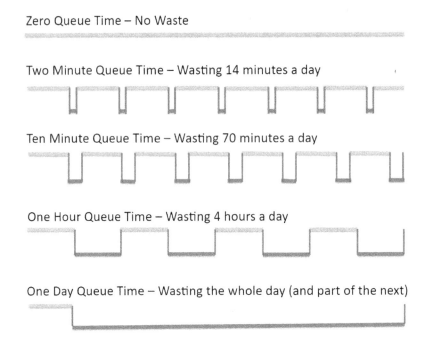

Zero Queue Time – No Waste

Two Minute Queue Time – Wasting 14 minutes a day

Ten Minute Queue Time – Wasting 70 minutes a day

One Hour Queue Time – Wasting 4 hours a day

One Day Queue Time – Wasting the whole day (and part of the next)

The first line represents the best case: there's no waiting, and we complete our work without delay.

The second line shows what happens when we work for an hour and then are blocked for two minutes. We waste a total of fourteen minutes per day.

The third line shows what happens when we work for an hour and then are blocked for ten minutes. We waste seventy minutes per day.

The fourth line shows us blocked every other hour, which means we waste half the day.

The last line indicates what happens when we work for an hour and then are blocked for the rest of the day. We've wasted almost an entire workday.

Imagine what would happen if we went to our manager and said, "Boss, I've just discovered a great way to waste most of the day!" Yet this is what's happening. (For the record, we don't suggest trying this with your boss.)

These are best-case scenarios because we don't count the additional delay caused by context switching. Switching comes with considerable overhead because it takes time to return to our flow state once it's interrupted. Nor do we consider the time to find the person who can unblock us and the inevitable back-and-forth with them.

We've also seen much worse scenarios where it sometimes took weeks to exit the queue. Of course, when delays of this magnitude happen, managers' instinctive reactions are "find something else to do," thereby adding to inventory. This approach doesn't solve the problem of queues. It merely solves the symptom of not being fully utilized. In our view, we should instead focus on solving the underlying problem: reducing the size and number of queues.

The chart below shows the dramatic effect of running our software engineering teams at full utilization. Queue lengths are exponential in systems such as software development that exhibit high variability. Going from 80% to 90% utilization more than doubles the queue size. Going from 90% to 95% more than doubles it again. At 100%, the wait time is infinite. In simple terms, the busier everyone is, the (infinitely) longer it takes to get things done.

Capacity Utilization vs Wait Time

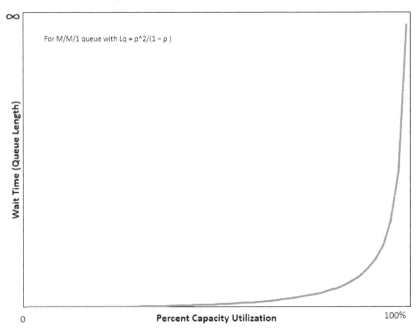

It's often worse than depicted here. The curve moves up and left with increasing system variability, and wait times approach infinity at much less than 100% utilization. In our view, this is the evidence we need to address the problems of queues.

Organizations are often reluctant to build slack into their systems because they want everyone fully utilized. Therefore, they can't absorb work surges, and their queues grow. In these environments, an effective strategy is to focus on reducing the number and length of queues instead of debating utilization [3]. We've found that it's a much easier approach for most organizations to accept.

Lastly, it's essential to understand that we aren't saying all queues must be removed regardless of cost. There's an economic trade-off involved [3].

However, we doubt the trade-off is relevant for most organizations, given that few are even aware of their queues.

3   Utilization versus Flow

By now, it might be evident that an inherent tension underlies the decision to adopt Software Teaming. This tension represents the tug-of-war between keeping everyone fully utilized versus maximizing the flow of the work.

As we've stated, many organizations default to maximizing utilization, disregarding flow. With Software Teaming, we choose to optimize for the flow of the work, not concerning ourselves with utilization. One way to view this inherent tension is with a simple chart that contrasts utilization with flow.

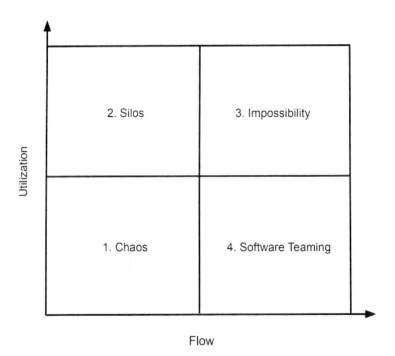

Modified from Modig and Ählstrom [4]

Increasing flow is shown on the horizontal axis while increasing utilization is displayed vertically [4]. We use four "zones" to define the different states organizations find themselves in.

Zone 1, in the lower left, is somewhat common. Much gets done, but it's often chaotic firefighting and other emergency work. Little of it is effective. Customers aren't happy, and neither are the workers. Our experience has been that these organizations struggle when faced with a more effective competitor.

Zone 2, in the upper left, is where most organizations aim. They want everyone fully tasked so they "get their money's worth." It's probably a philosophy derived from the dawn of the Industrial Revolution when machines were costly and had to be fully utilized to justify their investment. We think this approach continues in the modern era by replacing "expensive machines" with "expensive workers."

Everyone is always busy, and downtime is filled with "busy work." There's also much secondary work necessary because the "busy work" comes with overhead. Our experience has been that these types of organizations are sometimes unwilling to consider Software Teaming because it's such a radical change from their managerial belief that everyone must be fully utilized at all times.

There is often no responsibility for the overall quality because each silo manages only its own processes, and the overall system is poorly managed. In essence, we optimize local silos instead of the global system. This approach often means there's wasteful rework.

Work sits in queues while it waits for availability from the next silo. There are handoffs between silos, often with stage gates and management approvals required before the work can proceed. In Lean terms, the latency and management overhead is waste. In short, utilization comes at the cost of flow.

Zone 3, in the upper right corner, represents a perfect world with complete control over all possible variability. Manufacturers repetitively producing the same product can approach this state, but it's extraordinarily challenging in practice.

Indeed, combining high utilization with high flow is difficult, if not impossible [4]. It requires the ability to control all sources of variability. To us, it's extremely doubtful that software firms can ever achieve this state. There's far too much variability. Sources of it include

- Each customer need is different from the last and is inherently unpredictable.
- People do the work, not machines, and people are highly variable and unpredictable, unlike machines.
- Work arrives at an unpredictable rate.
- Work departs into Production at an unpredictable rate.
- Underlying technologies (languages, libraries, operating systems) change constantly. Their interaction is highly variable and sometimes fails.

Zone 4, in the lower right corner, is where Software Teaming exists. (It's important to understand that Zone 4 is not unique to Software Teaming. Any highly-collaborative work style belongs here as well.) We make a conscious choice to prioritize the flow of the work over the busyness of individuals. We accept that we must keep slack in the system, meaning that teams and individuals are not fully-utilized at any time. In this approach, work doesn't wait on people like in Zone 2. Instead, the work continues flowing because there's availability to absorb it, ensuring it always moves directly toward customer delivery.

We believe that when teams first adopt Software Teaming, there must be a learning phase to determine who should be included in the group to keep the work flowing. People might be added or removed until the balance is achieved. It's crucial that management give the team enough time and self-organizing freedom to discover this on their own and not interfere out of concern that "some people are idle."

We see an irony in being so focused on utilization that we separate our workers and fail to notice the resulting waste. In our view, the waste means that we aren't using our people efficiently, even though it's our stated goal. With Software Teaming, we focus on the flow of the work and aren't concerned with maximum busyness.

4   Productivity and Flow

Illustration © 2012 · Andrea Zuill

Now we can finally answer how five people at one computer can be productive. We simply changed the question to, "Are we effective?" That reoriented our worldview and led us to consider flow.

Flow means that work proceeds without any interruption from inception to completion. It allows us to steer toward a solution that rarely can be envisioned up front and must instead be found incrementally.

Flow with Software Development:
Each Story flows from "idea"
to delivered, working software
directly
without queueing,
inventory,
distraction,
interruption,
context switching,
or multitasking

In our experience, most organizations disregard flow and focus only on the utilization of their workers, ignoring inventory, queues, and the costs of delay. A full explanation of delay costs is beyond the scope of this book, but in simple terms, it represents the revenue lost by delaying the rollout of a feature. By delaying the rollout, we miss out on the income we could have received by deploying earlier.

Over time, this lost income can be substantial. Unfortunately, it's usually an invisible cost instead of a budgetary line item, which is why many organizations fail to consider it.

That's why we think it's an overly-simplistic view that would have us believe five people working independently are "getting more things done at the same time." It's simplistic because we disregard the costs of inventory waiting in queues.

We find that we reduce inventory and queues with Software Teaming's focus on flow. We also focus on fast feedback by quickly placing features into use. Rapid feedback is crucial in the uncertain world of software development. It provides powerful economic leverage but is rarely exploited [3].

We suspect we're more profitable when we focus on the flow of the work because we have greater throughput of income-generating material and spend less time engaged in wasteful "busy work." (Technically, we're probably using a Throughput Accounting approach. We won't go into the details here, nor should we, given that we aren't accountants.)

Contrast that to a more traditional approach where we focus primarily on worker costs and less on incurring the costs of creating queued inventory. We believe the traditional approach explains why managers focus on keeping workers busy and less on flow.

In summary, we discovered with Software Teaming that we were a much more effective team when working together than individually. We seek to get the best of each of us into everything we do instead of the most out of each person.

Our effectiveness comes from our ability to harness flow at the team and work-item levels, allowing us to produce a working product with minimal delay and waste. This approach answers the question, "How can we be effective with five people at one computer?" We're effective because we leverage the power of Psychological Flow, Team Flow, and Lean Flow.

A story from Kevin: As I look back on many years in the software industry, including stints as a senior manager, I wish I had done things differently. The executives I reported to optimized their system to make it easy to manage their workers and held me to account to ensure my staff was always fully utilized.

Since then, I often have wondered what things would have been like if we had structured the system differently. What if my bosses had said to me something like this (or better yet, if I had said it)?

"We expect you to optimize your division for delivering high-quality software into our customers' hands as quickly as possible. We think that will require a highly collaborative environment where your workers focus on working well together, so we want you to build highly-effective teams, not highly-busy individuals. The flow of their work items must never be interrupted. Anything that gets in their way needs to be your top priority. In fact, we want you to be able to see around corners so that nothing ever blocks them. You need to figure out the details of how to do this. That will make your job harder than how you've done it elsewhere, but that's what we require. It's your job to ensure it happens, and you will be accountable for that."

Alas, this never happened, but I suspect my teams would have been far more effective if it had. I also imagine my staff would have been happier, their product quality better, my division more profitable, and our customers would have been delighted with the outcome.

References

1. Csikszentmihalyi, Mihaly. Flow: The Psychology of Optimal Experience. New York: Harper and Row, 1990

2. van den Hout, Jef. The Conceptualization of Team Flow, The Journal of Psychology, Interdisciplinary and Applied, Volume 152, 2018, Issue 6.

3. Reinertsen, Donald. Principles of Product Development Flow, Celeritas, 2009.

4. Modig, Niklas, and Ählstrom, Pär. This Is Lean, Rheologica Publishing, Stockholm, 2020.

Part Six: Problems That Faded Away

Illustration © 2013 · Andrea Zuill

This part of the book addresses one of the fundamental discoveries of Software Teaming: how so many of our team's problems faded compared to other types of team arrangements we tried. When you finish this section, you should understand how we accomplished that.

1   The System Structure

Illustration © 2015 · Andrea Zuill

Is the work system structured how we want? Does it make it easy to get the good things we desire? Does it make the most effective use of our time and money? Well, let's take a trip and see what we find.

A Backpacking Trip

Let's take a backpacking trip to a beautiful, remote mountain lake. We'll hike as far as we can, enjoy a week in the wilderness, sleep under the stars, and refresh our souls.

We must bring food, clothes, a sleeping bag, and other necessities for sustenance and comfort. We want to enjoy as much time in the mountains as possible, so we must bring enough essentials, but we can only carry so much weight.

There are also some other things we need to bring: the backpack itself, food containers, and a sack for the sleeping bag. These items add weight without adding sustenance. If we can only carry fifty pounds, and our backpack weighs ten pounds, we'll need to leave behind ten pounds of food or other essentials, which means a shorter trip.

It would be great if we could make the trip without extra weight. We could bring more food and enjoy more of what we seek: hiking, fun, recreation, and nights under the stars. Unfortunately, we're stuck with the extra weight. We need the backpack, the food containers, and other items that add weight but aren't sustenance. We need this additional burden, but we want to minimize it if possible.

Management Overhead

When creating software, wouldn't it be great if we could spend all of our effort on the actual work of creating the software? These tasks include discovering customer needs, writing code, and verifying our features with the customer. But as with the backpacking trip, there's extra weight and burden.

We can think of this extra burden as Management Overhead. It's the effort required to manage the actual work of creating software. There's a substantial amount of this type of effort in most organizations.

Much of this effort concerns coordinating the work of people operating separately. This effort includes meetings, emails, follow-ups, status reports, code merges, code reviews, writing documents, scheduling work, and performance management. While we might need these items, finding a way to need less would be beneficial.

In short, the more time and money we spend managing the work, the less time and money we have for doing the work.

Working Well Together

What happens when we work well together, all day, every day? Much of the Management Overhead is no longer required. For example, there's no need for a meeting to discuss next week's work, no need for email communications about who should attend, and no need to manage the work assigned during the meeting.

When we all work together on the same thing simultaneously, many things improve drastically, and some of what's required to manage the work are no longer needed. Here are a few examples of things we've noticed:

- Out stories go from "start" to "finish" in a few hours. We get the story into Production and get rapid feedback on its value.
- Waiting for answers to questions happens much less. Everyone we usually require for answers sits with us.
- We get immediate and continuous design and code reviews with five or six sets of eyes on our code. Typical code smells like long methods and bad method names are significantly reduced, and quality skyrockets.
- We need fewer meetings.

Working separately, we get "the sum of the parts." Working together, well, this says it best:

"A system is never the sum of its parts. It is the product of the interactions of its parts."

Russell Ackoff

We didn't set out to solve specific problems that made it difficult to accomplish our work. What we did instead was deceptively simple. We learned to be observant and attentive to what was going well, working to Turn Up The Good. In so doing, we significantly reduced the amount of Management Overhead. Consequently, our backpack weighs two pounds when empty instead of ten.

It's essential to understand that Software Teaming isn't the sole contributing factor in lessening our Management Overhead. Software Teaming itself emerged from our attempts to Turn Up the Good of working in an Agile manner using techniques and practices like Test-Driven Development, small batches, frequent delivery of software into actual use, and simplicity. We consider these Agile practices as major contributors to reducing our Management Overhead.

What's Coming Up in the Next Chapters

In the following chapters, we share examples of problems that faded away for us when Software Teaming.

Our team retrospectives found numerous examples of "things that make it hard to work." We grouped them under the following categories.

- Communication Problems
- Decision-Making Problems
- Doing More than is Barely Sufficient
- Sustainability Erosion
- Thrashing of Team Members and the Team
- Politics
- Meetings

We describe examples from these categories in each of the upcoming chapters.

2 Problem: Faulty Communications

Illustration © 2012 - Andrea Zuill

Communication Problems are Pervasive, Numerous, and Paralyzing

There are many communication problems in software development worthy of an entire book on the subject, but we'll cover just a few here:

- Latency in Getting Answers to Questions
- Communication by Email
- Communication by Documentation

The Question Queue Time

It's common for developers working on a product to encounter a question they can't answer and must find someone who can. If the question blocks the person from further progress, they might need to switch to other work. Alternatively, they can make a "best guess" at the answer and confirm its accuracy later. There are different approaches to this, but nothing beats an immediate answer.

We typically have many questions throughout the development of a product, and it becomes a severe problem if the time spent waiting for answers is more than two or three minutes. Requiring two hours instead of two minutes to get an answer dramatically slows a product. Sometimes, it can take two or more days to get a response. Delays of this magnitude introduce vast amounts of wait time, destroying our ability to deliver working software "early and often."

For example, if you have ten questions and require two hours of waiting for each answer, that's twenty hours or half a workweek. If those same ten questions have a two-minute answer time, you have only twenty minutes of wasted time, and you can complete the feature by lunchtime. Imagine if it took two days to get each answer.

> *We call this the Question Queue Time: the amount of time we must wait before we get an answer to a question that is blocking us.*

We aren't getting anything done when we're blocked, which is wasteful idleness. It seems like we should always work on something and stay busy. We can't continue until we have an answer, so what can we do?

One typical way this is "solved" is by introducing other work (inventory) while we wait for the answer to the blocking question. This way, we can stay busy and productive. But we solve one problem by adding another: creating additional inventory. Inventory is work we've done but isn't yet delivering value to anyone. In Lean terms, inventory is waste and continues to be waste until it's delivered into use. (For further details on inventory and queues, see the Lean Flow section.)

Adding inventory brings its own problems: we now have to context switch between several stories. When the answer arrives to the blocking question, do we stop the new work and return to the original? If so, we'll need to switch back to the original context we were in before becoming blocked. We also need to consider the importance of the "new work." Are we ever going to finish it? Was it the next most important thing on the list or simply busy work to keep us from "wasting time?"

We've solved for "not being busy" rather than for not having a prompt answer. This strategy isn't a solution, however much it may feel like one. The allure of "staying busy" diverts us from seeking a solution to the real problem. Instead, we create an additional issue. By taking on "busy work" when we're blocked, we hide the queueing problem and mask it with an inventory problem.

With Software Teaming, a great deal of this problem merely faded away. All questions that another team member can resolve are always addressed immediately because the whole team works together on the same thing, at the same time, and in the same space. We have eliminated team member latency.

Initially, our Software Teaming group contained only programmers, eliminating the Question Queue Time between them. However, this exposed a more significant Question Queue Time: waiting on answers from people who weren't on our team. For us, this was the product owner, testers, database experts, and deployment experts. Over time, we added all of these people to the development team.

Here's the ideal we strive for: to have all the skills and knowledge we require on the team. While it may not always be possible to obtain everyone, it helps to pay attention and notice when there is repeated blocking. That's a sign that someone is missing from the team, and we should try to add them if possible.

Communication by Email

Asking questions by email is the last resort for us. In "Communication by Email," a simple question or request can take many emails back and forth as people clear up misunderstandings and move toward a shared understanding.

People become very careful when communicating by email because what they write might be held against them later. The more important the topic, the more cautious we become. We add other people to the email chain, such as our boss, so that we might protect ourselves.

With Software Teaming, we eliminate most email needs through continuous communication and rapid conversion of ideas into deployed, working code. Our preferred communication hierarchy is

1. Face-To-Face, Side-By-Side
2. Phone and screen share
3. Messaging apps
4. Email

We never move to the next level unless it's the only option to keep things moving.

Communication by Documentation

We write very little documentation. Documents lead to problems because they're open to misinterpretation. With more detail comes a greater possibility of misunderstanding. Documents are often written long before they can be validated. Usually, the document author is no longer available to help when questions arise.

We eliminate most Communication by Documentation through continuous communication. We rarely need a document to describe the functionality of the work because we work in small pieces and consistently achieve Lean Flow. We quickly validate our understanding by demonstrating and then deploying our completed code. We encourage our partners to create and use documents they feel they need. However, when it comes time to communicate their intent to us, we do it verbally and on the whiteboard in face-to-face interactions. This communication is quickly translated into code and verified the next day. Our work style makes this straightforward.

3   Problem: Issues with Decision Making

Illustration © 2013 · Andrea Zuill

Decisions Are a Good Thing

There are many decisions we need to make in software development. Some are more important than others. Here we address the nature of decision-making for the "more important" decisions.

Accountability

As typically used, accountability seems like a helpful idea. We want to make sure people do the right thing. Clearly, each of us should make good decisions about our area of expertise, and holding people accountable for those decisions seems like it provides better decisions.

Holding people accountable is a well-intentioned approach, and it likely makes people more diligent and careful in their decision-making. However, what if the side effects outweigh the possible benefits?

If something goes well, we want to know who to pat on the back and say, "job well done!" However, there's a more troubling side: if something goes wrong, we want to know who to hold accountable.

> **"We pay more attention to knowing who to blame in case we fail than in creating the conditions to succeed."**
>
> *Yves Morieux*

Is it possible we aren't getting the best results from this approach? Are we paying a higher cost than we realize?

Two Sides of the Same Problem

We cover two aspects here:

- There's often insufficient information and time available to decide with reasonable confidence, leading to a reluctance to commit.
- Once a decision is made, we might feel compelled to defend it. Perhaps even long after it's clear it's no longer defensible.

The second aspect (need to defend) reinforces the first aspect (reluctance to commit).

The Reluctance to Commit

We often don't have the information we need to make a decision when it's required. Once the decision is made, events unfold as they will, regardless of what we initially thought. Many things are simply out of our control.

Still, we're expected to make good decisions. We know we'll be held accountable for the decisions we make. How do we deal with this?

If we fear our decisions' consequences, we'll find ways to reduce that fear. Thus, we hold meetings, gather information, get allies, get advice, get approvals, and have things signed off by those impacted by the decisions.

Some of these activities, such as gathering information and thinking before we decide, are clearly helpful. As it's been said:

"In preparing for battle, I have always found that plans are useless, but planning is indispensable."

Dwight D. Eisenhower

Are we doing these things to help us make better decisions, or are we doing them to protect ourselves if the decision later turns out to have been wrong? We believe a significant amount of our efforts are intended to insulate ourselves from repercussions.

Need to Defend

Regardless of how carefully we research our decision, its value will inevitably decay with time because our environment changes. The original information loses its value as we continue working and discovering more information.

Once a decision is made, we often feel we must defend it. Defense is easy at first because the information is still fresh. However, the information becomes less relevant as it ages, weakening our defense. Once we defend a decision, it can become a vicious cycle. We feel more strongly that we must protect the original decision even as it becomes less and less valuable.

We often need to defend the original decision because of the possible consequences if others think it is wrong. There's also the "sunk cost fallacy:"

once we've invested in the decision, it's not easy to throw away the investment and start over.

Perhaps it's too easy to find reasons for continuing a decision even after it seems we should abandon it. This practice is nicely described in a quote from Ben Franklin:

"So convenient a thing to be a reasonable creature, since it enables one to find or make a reason for everything one has a mind to do."

Benjamin Franklin

What's Wrong with This System?

There are numerous problems with this system. We're probably wasting time and money, both in making the decision and clinging to it after it has outlived its usefulness.

We're surrendering the right to evolve and adapt. If we're to be held accountable for something, perhaps it should be for maintaining the ability to revisit and change our decisions frequently.

"When the facts change, I change my mind. What do you do, sir?"

attributed to John Maynard Keynes

How Software Teaming Helps with Decision-Making

Wouldn't it be nice to find a way to make good decisions without having sufficient information? That may not be possible. But with Software Teaming, we work on one thing at a time. This practice means that many decisions don't need to be made until we actually do the work surrounding the decision. We find that doing the work exposes what work must be done.

> *It's in the doing of the work that we discover the work that we must do.*

Delaying decisions until we do the surrounding work makes the decisions much easier because we have the information we need to decide. We think of this as "just-in-time" decision-making.

The results of our decisions are validated quickly, often in actual use.

Much less information gathering and analysis have to be done because the most recently validated work item informs the decisions we need to make for the next work item. We also require far fewer decisions with this approach.

> *We no longer need to make many of the decisions we previously needed to make.*

Because we work in small steps, our decisions are easy to undo. We can quickly prove or disprove any idea and use the feedback to modify our decision instantly. We steer toward a solution, validating as we go, rather than attempting to envision one in advance when we have little validation available.

Additionally, since everyone is involved in creating and reviewing our decisions, there's no one to whom we must defend them. We all own them.

Lastly, it's easier to reverse a decision when we're all part of making it.

4 Problem: Doing More Than What's Barely Sufficient

Illustration © 2013 - Andrea Zuill

Should We Ever do More than Enough?

When creating software, doing the bare minimum of design, code, and features simplifies the application, making it easier to use, maintain, and enhance. In Agile, this is one of the principles:

"Simplicity–the art of maximizing the amount of work not done–is essential."

Principles behind the Agile Manifesto

In Lean terms, this is related to overproduction, which is considered a waste. In Lean Software Development, it appears as additional processes and features. We hear words like "Gold-Plating," "Software Bloat," and "Feature Creep." This overproduction isn't just the number of features but also the processes for creating the software.

A Swedish term sums it up nicely: Lagom. As we understand it, this means "just right, sufficient, adequate, enough." Whenever we do more than "just right," we've done too much.

Examples of "Too Much"

Doing more than is barely sufficient is often a problem. Here are some examples where you might see "Too Much" done to solve problems.

Too Many Features

The user experience should be intuitive, simple, and straightforward. Each additional feature adds complication and expense, making the application harder to maintain and enhance.

While having many features seems wonderful, it isn't always worthwhile. It's a difficult, endless balancing act deciding which features to include and which to omit.

Bloated Feature Implementation

Each feature has the same problem. It's common to hear, "we need all of this feature, or it isn't worth doing at all." It's hard, if not impossible, to prove that we need every part of it.

What's the problem with bloated features? As with too many features, each feature part adds complication and expense, making the application harder to maintain, enhance, and use.

Over-Design, Hacking Things Together

It's common to see code quickly blossom into "way too much." We often see software that's over-designed for its intended use and unnecessarily complex. Once in place, overdesign tends to resist simplification.

Deadlines inevitably loom. When they do, complexity makes changes hard, and we sometimes end up hacking things together, usually with a promise to "fix it later."

The more code we write, the more we need to maintain. When that code is over-complicated, we make it harder to change later.

Test Bloat

Like features and code, tests can become complicated, convoluted, and full of cruft and deadwood. Test bloat can make it more challenging to change feature code.

How Software Teaming has Helped

We didn't plan directly to solve any of the above problems. However, after beginning Software Teaming, we found that many problems simply faded away.

Software Teaming naturally amplifies "maximizing the amount of work not done." Perhaps the most powerful feature is the Lean Flow nature of the work. For our use, Lean Flow means we all work on one small feature at a time from start to finish and deliver it to the customer before starting on another feature.

Here are some things we found while Software Teaming that helped us minimize the problems listed above.

Barely Sufficient Number of Features

The problem of "Too many features" faded away for us. With Software Teaming, we go quickly from idea to deployed feature. Deploying provides feedback, telling us whether the feature is useful or not. From there, we decide on the next potentially useful thing to work on. We only work on one thing at a time, so we become accomplished at steering towards that next thing.

Also, because everyone works together, we have a smooth, rapid delivery and deployment cycle. This working model removes the typical blocking that occurs on products. (For example, "I'm blocked waiting on an answer from so and so.") As a result, we get feedback quickly telling us when we're "done." When the remaining features don't seem important, we're done for the moment and can work on another product.

Barely Sufficient Feature Implementation

It can be a great advantage to do as little work as possible on a feature, put it into use, quickly get feedback, and prove or disprove its usefulness. Rapid feedback allows us to discover what else is needed, growing it until it's "just enough."

With Software Teaming, we work with the product expert, users, and testers as part of the team. We can make rapid choices about the smallest deliverable version of the part we're working on.

Working this way allows us to slice off and implement parts of a feature to find what's most useful. We continue slicing and delivering until what's left doesn't seem important, and we can move on to the next feature.

The customer might not be interested in another feature that solves a small percentage of the problem. In that case, we have sufficiently solved the problem.

Typically, we "grow into" barely sufficient rather than "cutting back" to barely sufficient. You can't "un-spend the money" if you're cutting back. "Growing into" features minimizes waste because we aren't doing all the work before we get useful feedback.

Barely Sufficient Code

With Software Teaming, we have all eyes on the code, and every team member is mindful of finding the most direct and understandable solution. For us, code issues such as over-design, long methods, and large classes just faded away.

With everyone working together, we get an enhanced focus on simplicity and clarity, making the code easier to understand. Our code contains the best of each of us. The good is amplified, and the bad is minimized.

Barely Sufficient Tests

Just like feature code, unit tests can grow into a problem. We must stay vigilant to prevent a mass of unreadable or incomprehensible unit tests. With Software Teaming, the whole team focuses on the simplicity and quality of the unit tests. With this approach, we get sufficient tests, just what we need, and no more.

Conclusion

Our experience with Software Teaming has allowed us to reduce the time, effort, and money we spend solving business problems.

We've found that Software Teaming promotes a Lean Flow approach, requiring "barely sufficient" effort because:

- We work together on only one thing at a time.
- We get done sooner without blocking and waiting for answers.
- We have short delivery cycles providing rapid feedback.
- We steer toward a solution as our understanding of the problem and solution grows.
- We omit things that we would keep in other approaches.

We spend the right amount of money to solve the right amount of the problem. In short, we discover what's "just enough."

5 Problem: Sustainability Erosion

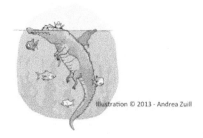

Illustration © 2013 - Andrea Zuill

The Alligator in the Pond

There's a common problem in software engineering. It's a problem where software steadily increases in complexity and instability, eventually becoming unmaintainable. The term we often hear describing this issue is Technical Debt. However, as formally defined, Technical Debt represents a different problem. To better explain this problem of increasingly unmaintainable code, we introduced the term Sustainability Erosion in Part Three.

Sustainability Erosion is a progressive and debilitating disease in software engineering that quickly destroys our ability to deliver value sustainably. It manifests as unnecessary complexity in the code that makes it harder to work on than it would otherwise be.

Once we allow this complexity to exist, it becomes easier to accumulate more. If it's allowed to grow unchecked, it can act like an anchor that slows or prevents forward progress. The codebase becomes so problematic that even minor changes become risky, time-consuming gambles.

Although the term is new, the concept of Sustainability Erosion is well known. One way to think about it might be "The Alligator in the Pond." It starts small, but it grows over time. Eventually, it becomes enormous. Still, we only see a bit of it peeking out of the pond, perhaps just its eyes and nose. But it has become dangerous and will devour us sooner or later. Getting rid of it by then is a vast and risky job.

It Faded Away

We didn't set out to solve our Sustainability Erosion problems with Software Teaming. We found it simply faded away because we automatically developed a mindset of Clean Code and simplicity.

The Software Teaming Mindset of Clean Code

It can be easy to take shortcuts and convince ourselves that our code doesn't add to Sustainability Erosion when working alone, even if we harbor inner misgivings. We often say, "Well, it could be better, but it'll do for now. Other work is urgently needed. I'll come back to this later and clean it up."

Unfortunately, given the demands on our time, "later" often never comes, and the code we wrote adds to the product's Sustainability Erosion. Alternatively, we may not know that our code adds to the problem. It's an innocent oversight that periodically happens to all of us.

However, when Software Teaming, it's much harder to leave this kind of code in place because addressing Sustainability Erosion is part of the work, not a distraction. Someone on the team will likely say, "Hey, everyone, I think we should clean this up now, or it will make things harder for us later." Also, innocent oversights are less likely to happen when multiple people continuously inspect the code.

We collectively encourage each other to keep our code in great shape. Whenever someone senses that something is more challenging than it should be, they'll mention it, and we'll take the time to see if there's some hidden complexity slowing us down.

> *With Software Teaming, we continuously review our designs and inspect our code, reducing our Sustainability Erosion.*

Perhaps this is due to a team's collective watchfulness compared to working alone. It's harder to rationalize risky code when everyone is responsible for the well-being of each other. We're constantly on the lookout for things that will bite us later. When Software Teaming, our mindset is to say, "let's fix it now" instead of "we'll fix it later." We aim to make tomorrow's work as easy as today's and, preferably, easier.

The Many Forms of Sustainability Erosion

Sustainability Erosion can take many forms. We'll look at some examples and how Software Teaming helps us avoid it.

Duplicate Code and Hidden Abstractions

Duplicate code is one factor contributing to Sustainability Erosion. While it's not always a problem, it often is. Unfortunately, it's not always obvious.

One example is when we have two different solutions for the same or a very similar problem. This issue often happens when several programmers have individually coded the solutions in isolation. There's a pattern to be found. But developers working separately typically don't have an opportunity to notice patterns, either in the problems they're working on or in their solutions. There's a hidden abstraction present that isn't immediately obvious.

While a code review might reveal this, reviews are done "after the fact," and the pattern will likely remain hidden unless the same person reviews both solutions. Additionally, dissimilar solutions to similar problems are often sufficiently different that the commonality isn't easily noticed, even when the same reviewer reviews both solutions.

We work on one story at a time with Software Teaming. The whole team knows each story, and each person helps devise every solution. The chance of noticing that something we're working on today is similar to something we worked on recently is much more likely than when working in silos. For example:

Mary remarks, *"This reminds me of some problem we've solved recently."*

"Yeah, I remember that," says Gonzo, *"What was that?"*

Pat has an epiphany, *"Oh yeah, this is like the transaction pattern we worked with last month for the mailing module, and I know right where that is."*

We've had many instances, even months later, where someone on the team recognizes something "seems familiar" about a story. The team's group memory allows us to locate the previous solution quickly. We can then investigate approaches that enable us to abstract the commonality and create simpler solutions with less duplication.

> *Group memory forms in a Software Teaming group in a way that doesn't happen when we work separately.*

Group memory is one way we prevent the rise of problem code and, in effect, keep the alligator small.

Inherited Problems

We've shown how Software Teaming can minimize the accrual of Sustainability Erosion. What about the situation when you inherit it? What if the alligator is already large and dangerous? How many of us can relate to this story of Beth, the programmer?

Beth is happily coding away just before lunch and thinking of the delicious noodles she's about to enjoy at her favorite local restaurant. Suddenly her manager Richard appears.

Richard: *Hey, Beth, we have an emergency. We just signed a client that requires a change to the Wonky feature in our Perambulator app. Remember that feature? The architect worked on it last year and built it over a weekend.*

Beth: *Yeah, I remember that. Wasn't it kind of problematic? Didn't we have to spend a lot of time rebooting its server because it leaked so much memory that it crashed all the time?*

Richard: *Yeah, but it's solid now. We haven't had any problems in a long time.*

Beth: *Well, I guess I should go talk to the architect just to get up to speed on it.*

Richard: *He quit last week. By the way, we need this done by the end of the month. That's when we promised the client it would be ready. I'll check in every day to see how you're doing.*

Beth: *Oh.*

At this point, Beth has a vague foreboding of imminent doom. Perhaps something like an engineer on the Titanic asking, "What was that noise? Did we just hit something?"

Beth reluctantly decides to skip the noodles and grabs a snack from the vending machine, eating it at her desk while digging around to find the Wonky code. She finds the project, and it has just one class called "Wonky." Hmm, that's odd, just one class. She opens it and sees the first method called "DoWonk3". She scrolls through the method to see what it does. And scrolls. And scrolls, and scrolls some more. Finally, after 10,321 lines, she reaches the end of the method. And of the class.

"That's it?!! Just one method? Oh no. Well, maybe it isn't too bad. Let's see what's in here."

Beth examines the method more slowly. Partway through it, the code indentation causes the code to disappear off the right side of her screen. There are so many levels of nested IF statements and embedded SWITCH statements that her monitor isn't wide enough to show them all.

Utterly dejected, Beth wonders what to do next. Perhaps, she thinks, the asteroid that wiped out the dinosaurs has a cousin, and it's due for a visit before the end of the month. Alas, no, it looks like vending machine lunches for the rest of the month. And some long nights and weekends. Sigh.

Sound familiar? It probably does. This kind of code can be frightening to handle by yourself. There are hundreds, perhaps thousands, of logical paths in it. What if you miss one? If you're lucky, it will fail upon deployment, and there will be a meaningful error message and a way to reproduce it. If you're unlucky, it will fail long after being deployed. By this time, you've lost memory of its logic, and there will be a 3 AM call like this:

Beth (sleepily, fumbling for her glasses in the dark): *Hello? Who is this?*

Carl: *Hey, Beth, it's Carl from the Operations Team. We just got a call from our client's IT department telling us they didn't get their Perambulator report this morning.*

Beth: *Did you check to see if the file is in their directory?*

Carl: *Yeah, there's nothing there except yesterday's report in the Archives subdirectory.*

Beth: *What do the logs say? Any errors or other info?*

Carl: *No, they don't show anything. I can see where it ran yesterday, but there's no log entry for today and no error of any kind.*

Beth: *Great. OK, I'll look into it now. Let me start some coffee first.*

Carl: *Thanks, Beth. Please hurry and call me as soon as you have a status update. They're really angry about this, and their IT department is pinging me every 15 minutes wanting an answer.*

This scenario might sound familiar. Yet, maybe there's a better approach than struggling through these situations alone.

Imagine if you could take away the fear of tackling these long methods. Imagine if you could have others help you unravel it, and you felt confident in your changes. Imagine a Software Teaming group working on it. It might look like this:

Beth: *What's this SWITCH block supposed to do? For some reason, it checks if the variable wonk3 equals the variable xx7.*

Gonzo: *Well, it looks like higher up in the code, there's another SWITCH statement that sets wonk3 to a date.*

Pat: *Hmm, the code does some date math on xx7, just above the comparison with wonk3.*

Beth: *Oh, I see. It allows the Wonk to run on leap days. Otherwise, the client won't get their report on that day. Let's extract that into its own method, give it a good name, write a test for it, and get the code to work. That way, we won't get the dreaded 3 AM call from Carl on the Operations Team.*

Of course, there's no guarantee that a Software Teaming group won't miss something tricky in the code, as Beth did in the first example. But it's less likely when multiple sets of eyes carefully evaluate the code, continuously review the work, and focus on improving the code.

Also, as the code knowledge grows within the team, there's less pressure on just one individual to accomplish everything without any mistakes. For example, after a long Software Teaming session, Beth feels tired.

Beth: *Guys, I'm exhausted and not keeping up with everyone. Mind if I take a break and get some coffee and fresh air?*

Software Teaming Group: *No problem. We'll continue working while you're out. We'll get you up to speed on what we've done when you return.*

While Beth takes a break, the work continues, unlike the situation where Beth would be working alone.

The alligator had grown large and frightening, but the Software Teaming group collaborated to bring it back down to size. This collaboration is preferable to facing a large alligator all alone.

Conclusion

While we didn't set out to solve our Sustainability Erosion problems, working together allowed us to exercise the discipline needed to eliminate a significant amount of it. Could we have accomplished this without Software Teaming? Perhaps. There are many ways to eliminate or reduce Sustainability Erosion. But, we found it automatically happened once we began Software Teaming.

6 Problem: Thrashing

Illustration © 2012 - Andrea Zuill

Distractions, Context Switching, Interruptions: This is Thrashing

Our first understanding of "thrashing" was the sound from an overworked hard drive. When a computer is thrashing, it can't perform critical operations because resources are exhausted or too limited. A thrashing system has come to a halt.

Thrashing of Programmers

There are other uses of this concept in software development. Our focus is on the thrashing of the people and teams doing software development.

Thrashing is the interruption, redirection, or distraction of a team or team member from their current work, reducing their effectiveness in accomplishing that work. Here are some examples:

- Being asked to switch from one task to another
- Questions that interrupt our focus while programming
- Emergency work
- Meetings
- Waiting for answers to blocking questions
- Playing multiple roles
- Moving people from team to team ("load balancing")

Who Gets Thrashed?

While we're all vulnerable to being thrashed, a few team members are the most likely candidates. It's frequently the most knowledgeable people. These are the go-to people for many aspects of our work. The skills that make them valuable to the team also make them valuable to everyone else. Here are some common thrashing targets:

- The "Lone Expert." The one person who knows a given functionality. They're the only one who can help in that area and are redirected to that work whenever the need arises.
- Those who can't say no. Regardless of how much it will disrupt them, they agree to help.
- Anyone assigned to more than one team. Team members from both teams feel free to interrupt them at any time.

Why is Thrashing Harmful?

Thrashing can cause many problems, which may not be immediately apparent. Here are some examples:

- The introduction of additional inventory.
- The waste of work we begin, drop, and restart later.
- The disruption to the flow of the team's work.
- Everyone is blocked when the team's "go-to" person is pulled away.
- Quality suffers when we lose focus on our work.
- The unfinished work of "thrashed" team members becomes a blocking point for other team members.

How it Faded Away for Us

We were surprised that thrashing almost immediately evaporated once we started Software Teaming.

Most of our work is quickly finished when focusing on one small thing at a time, limiting the window for interruptions.

When the product expert is working with us as a team member, they know they can introduce our next work item within a few hours. There's no need to interrupt current work.

When someone brings us an emergency, the whole team scrutinizes it for relevance. Sometimes the crisis can wait or be resolved with a simple workaround. If it can wait, it's added to our workflow as the next item once we complete the current one. This approach often results in a faster and better resolution than assigning a single team member to work on it alone.

When something requires immediate attention, we drop everything and take care of it quickly. With the whole team's attention on it, few emergencies consume much of our time. When we resume the interrupted work, it's easy for us to get back into the flow. Since we're in a Team Flow, we remind ourselves of what we were doing, where we were, and what we were thinking or considering. We quickly regain our context.

In some uncommon cases, we found it better to have one person split off from the team and address an emergency. We're a bit less effective without that team member, but we can continue working without losing our Team Flow. In these cases, the team decides who's the best person to handle something. It isn't arbitrary or determined by someone else. We find it highly beneficial when the team is allowed to decide how to do the work. We see much better results this way.

> *The people doing the work can best determine how to do that work.*

When a non-emergency request arrives, it goes on our workboard in an area called "New Items." As soon as we finish our current task, we look at what's new and decide what action to take next. The task in question can be moved into current work or placed in a queue of "Upcoming Possibilities."

Having a team workspace limits access to individual team members. Anyone visiting our area works with the team, reducing trivial interruptions. Additionally, the whole team watches for unnecessary interruptions, quickly assessing almost any request for importance and urgency.

7   Problem: Politics

Illustration © 2012 · Andrea Zuill

Many Faces of Politics

There are many faces of politics in business. We'll cover a few things that are relevant to the improvements we've seen when Software Teaming.

We're referring specifically to "office politics." In some companies, the system in place creates an unhealthy environment. People feel compelled to work in a competitive rather than collaborative way. This way of work leads to decisions that help one individual but might be at the expense of others.

We believe that office politics result from a management system prioritizing competition over collaboration among workers. No matter how well-intentioned, it's difficult for individuals to overcome the system's effects. Deming made a strong point about this:

"A bad system will beat a good person every time."

W. Edwards Deming

Nonetheless, we were surprised to see one of these problems fade away when we started Software Teaming. Let's look more closely.

Problem: A Disincentive to Help Others

In software development, we often work as part of a team. However, we typically work as independent team members. We're then evaluated on accomplishing our work rather than the team's. This system inadvertently incentivizes us to be less helpful than we otherwise want to be.

Helping someone else takes time away from our own work and requires context switching to the other person's flow. We lose our own context and flow, which takes considerable time to regain once we finish helping. Of course, this works in both ways. When we need a teammate's help, we break their flow. Consequently, we negatively affect both people.

How is this politics?

The system's setup puts us in a double bind: we want to help but are under pressure to get our work done. A teammate's help request requires us to decide between completing our own work versus helping someone else. We're forced to make an inherently political decision whether or not we intend it to be. While this isn't the system's intention, it's often the result.

It Faded Away

This problem faded away for us because, with Software Teaming, everyone works together on the same thing, at the same time, on the same computer. We aren't judged individually on our output. What's important is the outcome of the team's efforts. It's never a distraction to answer a question because it's about the very thing we're working on. We're free of the double bind.

Again, we didn't plan to solve this problem. It literally evaporated as soon as we started Software Teaming.

8 Problem: Meetings

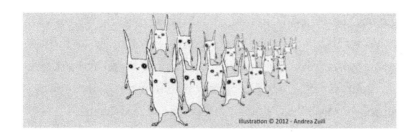

illustration © 2012 - Andrea Zuill

"Please, Sir, I Want Some More Meetings."

While Oliver Twist actually wanted more gruel, we meet few people who ask for more meetings.

It sometimes feels like we're in meetings much of the day, often finding ourselves in meetings with seemingly no purpose and no beneficial outcome. We have several options to improve things when we see unhelpful meetings. One is to change the meetings, so they're more effective. Another is to accomplish the same purpose in other ways, so the meetings aren't necessary.

Meetings are often an intermediate step. Meetings aim to set up "actual work." If we take a different approach to the actual work, then "setting up" wouldn't be needed, and we can skip the meeting.

In the typical meeting pattern, people gather, share information, make decisions, assign work, and leave to either do the work or manage it. We believe this often results in harmful separation of work and knowledge-creation from decision-making.

After a meeting, those who have questions are separated from those who can provide answers. Those who can validate things are separated from those who create things to be validated. So, while people might work together for a short time and be somewhat aligned at the meeting's end, it's a very fragile alignment. We start diverging quickly or even immediately.

The gather, share, decide, assign, and disperse meeting style isn't a very collaborative way to work. It often requires extra work to manage the agreed-upon work from the meeting. Additional tasks and artifacts are needed to address this: agendas, meeting minutes, follow-ups, email communications, checklists, status reports, and spreadsheets.

After the meeting, any questions, clarifications, and validations require tracking down the right person to help. Communication is put into queues and done via emails, phone calls, and follow-on meetings.

With Software Teaming, our entire day is a working meeting. It's more like a workshop than a meeting because we're working together, not merely meeting. We share information, decide what to do, do it together, verify our understanding, then deploy it. Over and over.

We collaborate and remain in alignment all day long. Any questions are answered immediately. Work is validated as we go and put into use as quickly as possible, often on the same day it's coded, allowing users to verify its value.

We find very little need for planning meetings, stand-ups, reviews, and other meetings that plague the typical development organization.

Part Seven: The Last Word

Illustration © 2013 - Andrea Zuill

This part of the book answers common questions we hear when people first start Software Teaming and presents our closing remarks. When you finish this section, you should have answers to common questions and understand our opinions on Software Teaming's value.

1   Frequently Asked Questions

Illustration © 2014 - Andrea Zuill

There are often many questions that arise when considering Software Teaming. It's a different way of working for most of us, and there's much to consider. We answer common questions in this chapter.

What's the ideal number of team members?

This question is often asked, but there's no definitive answer.

When we first discovered Software Teaming, we were a team with six members. We didn't need to consider the ideal number. We just worked with the people already on the team. We included the product owner or business expert as part of the team whenever they were available. This method worked well for us, and we created great software daily.

Expanding the Team

Over time, we occasionally found situations where we had a larger-than-usual problem. These problems required expertise from a wide range of people we didn't have on the immediate team. We might need a business expert who understood the process we were automating, a finance expert, end users, programmers from other teams, managers, a network expert, and anyone directly affected by the functionality being worked on.

We never took an exact headcount, but we sometimes needed up to fourteen people to handle these complex workflows. The work still progressed well when we required so many people.

Our purpose was to get input from everyone who might help us determine the right things to work on. Not everybody needed to code at the keyboard, but they were welcome if they wished.

Sometimes we had a very small team. Perhaps someone was out of town or home sick, and only three or four of us were available. It didn't seem to be a problem. We usually understood our work well enough to keep moving forward.

So while the minimum was three, and the maximum we ever had was around fourteen, we never considered any specific maximum limit. We found that things worked nicely if everyone involved could help us steer, code, and discover a good solution.

We created a heuristic for expanding the team: if we can't answer our own question, it indicates we're missing knowledge on the team. We can obtain knowledge by adding someone to the team or learning it ourselves.

Shrinking the Team

Occasionally, a team member felt they weren't contributing enough or weren't learning anything useful. In that case, they often preferred to leave the team briefly and work on something worthwhile.

We created a simple heuristic to capture this concept, using it as our guideline: if you feel you're contributing or learning, you might as well stay with the team. Otherwise, you can temporarily move off the team and work on something alone or with a pair.

Since our workspace included a nearby area where someone could temporarily work solo or with a pair, they were close enough to be called back to the team if needed. We often found that we had a question for the person shortly after they left the team. Being nearby, they were instantly available to return and help us.

If someone consistently feels they aren't contributing or learning, they can decide to remove themselves from the team and permanently join another.

This idea is known as the "Law of Mobility" in the Open Space Un-Conference community. Harrison Owen, the originator of the Open Space concept, explains it like this:

"If at any time during our time together you find yourself in any situation where you are neither learning nor contributing, go someplace else."

Harrison Owen

The expanding and shrinking heuristics make it easy for the team members to self-adjust to the right mix of people for just about any size problem.

What if I'm a slow typist, even though I've tried for years to get faster? How can I be a Driver? I'll hold everyone back.

It's important to note that the Driver is usually only typing for a few minutes and won't hold back the team for long. Indeed, if you observe solo programmers, you might notice that they spend little time typing and far more thinking. Programming generally doesn't consist of typing in continuous code streams, so a slow typist might have little impact.

Of course, if you're genuinely worried, why not express that to the team? It may not pose the problem you imagine. Perhaps the team will say, "No worries. We'll just be a little slower when you're the Driver. It won't be a problem." Or perhaps the team will gladly consider some other solution, such as finding a way to help you improve your typing skill. Maybe you'll improve with the team supporting you. Perhaps you could skip every other turn as a Driver.

Each team can work out the best approach. It's helpful to realize that the team shares a problem and self-determines a solution.

What happens when there are extroverts on the team? Will they push the other team members aside? What if I'm shy and introverted? How can I fit in with the team and give my input?

This issue will be a problem if it isn't recognized and addressed. The first thing to note here is that we can all benefit by being more thoughtful when sharing our ideas. In the moment's enthusiasm, it's easy to blurt out a thought and interrupt someone else who's already speaking. If the speaker is introverted, they may stop sharing and allow the other person to talk, thus gaining one voice but losing another. We help alleviate this by choosing to listen before we speak. This skill takes practice and mindfulness because it often doesn't come naturally.

As teams, we need to allow the more introverted members to have their say. Otherwise, it can be easy for the extroverts to dominate the conversation and thereby accidentally silence introverts. Teams benefit if they learn to listen for the more quiet voices.

For example, after finishing a discussion, it can be helpful for one team member to say to another, "I noticed you started to say something. Do you still want to express that idea?" At this point, the rest of the team listens while the teammate expresses their idea. Perhaps the team may hear something that advances the solution. Of course, the team member is free to reply, "No, my idea is covered in the solution we have." or "Not now, perhaps later." Either way, the team must find a way to allow everyone an equal voice. In our view, we benefit from hearing all voices.

What's the maximum time someone should serve as the Driver before switching? What if the Driver role lasted all day or a week?

There are no strict rules here. Every team will probably find something that works best for them and might be different from others. We experimented and found that rotating every seven minutes worked well, but we tried everything from four to fifteen minutes. Nothing magical about the time interval we chose makes it a universal standard. It just worked well for us.

We've seen other teams use different arrangements, such as rotating every hour, on every story, or whenever someone felt it was their turn to be the Driver or they no longer wanted to be the Driver.

Again, each team can experiment and find what works best for them. One thing to consider is that a greatly-extended Driver period might cause the Driver to drift slowly away from a conceptual understanding of the software. The team can self-moderate to avoid this by allowing the Driver to rotate if they feel they're starting to drift.

Should the Driver sit in front of all the Navigators or the other way around? How about putting the Navigators in a semicircle around the Driver?

Again, every team will find what works best for them, but we found it worked well to sit in a semicircle behind the Driver or side-by-side with the Driver. We've seen one team project the code onto the ceiling while the Navigators leaned back in bean-bag-style chairs and the Driver worked from a laptop. There are too many options to limit ourselves.

What happens when there are different skill levels among the team? Won't the ideas of the advanced programmers dominate the solutions?

If skill levels differ among team members, it might actually help the overall effectiveness and advancement of the team. We find that a skill difference amplifies learning across the entire team. Of course, proper listening skills must be in place. The mix of skills allows the more junior programmers to absorb the expertise of the more advanced members. It might also challenge the expert members to new ways of thinking and help liberate them from cognitive ruts that can form over time.

We sometimes found it helpful to try the junior programmer's idea first when there were differing ideas about how to proceed with a given task. We often learned something new, and the solution was simple and effective.

Trying the junior programmer's approach also avoids the problem where a more senior programmer doesn't spend the requisite time to explain their idea and instead grabs the keyboard, quickly "coding it for you." In that situation, we risk only one person understanding the approach, losing team review, and possibly introducing faulty code. Does this slow down the team? Perhaps, but slowing things might be a good idea if it prevents introducing a bad idea.

Why is it essential to be able to explain our ideas? For example, why should an expert programmer need to present ideas to junior programmers? We believe that explaining our ideas requires us to understand them before implementing them. The brilliant physicist Richard Feynman, a Nobel laureate, was once asked to explain a complex physics problem to first-year physics students. He tried but failed, providing this telling rationale:

"You know, I couldn't do it. I couldn't reduce it to the freshman level. That means we really don't understand it."

Richard Feynman

What if I can't keep up with the speed of the programming? How will I be able to master the codebase if I'm falling behind in my understanding? When I code alone, I have time to let the ideas sink in.

This issue can happen, but your skills and abilities will grow as you work with the team. With time you'll be able to keep up, gaining skills with this new model of working and learning. Understanding how the code works will naturally occur as you gain experience on the team and time in the code. It's important to know that as a Software Teaming group member, you don't always have to understand everything at all times. Other team members will understand the parts that you don't.

This approach is the idea of a "collective brain:" the knowledge is spread across the team. Some code features might drift past you, but there will still be other parts you understand. With more engagement and time, you'll gain mastery of the code.

Additionally, it can be easier to understand complex code when working on a team because there are other team members to help explain it. It's helpful to leverage multiple people's power when deciphering complicated code. If you're still lost, why not bring this to the team's attention and ask for help? Helping each other is one of the key responsibilities of a Software Teaming group.

There's a benefit in asking for help understanding the code: it requires the rest of the team to explain it. The explanation may expose problems that weren't apparent beforehand. Also, if the team finds it can't be explained, we may not completely understand the code, triggering the need for a better understanding.

Can you still do Software Teaming if you can't do it all the time? Can you do it only for occasions when it seems critical?

Sure! No rule states any organization that considers Software Teaming must have every team do it at all times. Some may find it most helpful when their teams use Software Teaming only for the most critical problems, such as addressing complicated and messy legacy code (think about that enormous JavaScript file everyone is afraid to touch). Or perhaps there's a user story that must meet strict, complex business rules, and it would be much better to have a Software Teaming group work on it.

Alternatively, some organizations may find Software Teaming so much to their liking that they always choose to do it. That works too. The takeaway is that each organization can experiment and see what works best for them.

We suggest that if you decide to do Software Teaming, you do it often enough to become proficient.

How can we do Software Teaming with remote teams?

For details on Remote Software Teaming, see the Remote Software Teaming chapter.

Can we use Software Teaming in large organizations?

Certainly. We know of many large organizations with teams doing Software Teaming.

There's usually room for experimentation in large organizations. A few teams can try Software Teaming and see how it goes. When first experimenting with Software Teaming, it's helpful for the team to pay attention to the experiment, adjusting their approach as needed. Paying attention is an essential part of continuous improvement.

We think Software Teaming works best when it's voluntary. We suggest allowing individuals to move onto or off Software Teaming groups as they see fit.

Where do our testers and other specialists fit?

In our view, testers aren't separate from others working on the product. The testers' skills, knowledge, and mindset are essential to the team's daily work.

Testers are often the only people on the team who deeply understand how end-users will use the application. This understanding is an essential viewpoint for the team. In our approach, a tester isn't waiting for something to test. They help create testable software that's continuously tested as it's developed.

Taking this one step further, we tend toward an unconventional view we believe is highly effective. We think specialists such as testers, database experts, and product managers are more effective when they're members of the Software Teaming group.

When all the specialists are on the team, we have better flow and make better decisions than when working in silos. This approach also distributes critical skills and knowledge across the team, removing the risk of losing a key person. We understand this philosophy might not be for everyone, but our experience with it has been positive.

How can we do individual performance reviews when everyone is on a team?

Our response to this may be surprising because we aren't fans of performance reviews. We avoid them because we believe they're fraught with problems and often do more harm than good. This belief isn't just ours. The celebrated management consultant W. Edwards Deming had a dim view of performance reviews.

"The annual appraisal of performance or the so-called merit system: Of all the forces of destruction that have beset American industry, this one has dealt the most powerful blow. It destroys people, our most important asset."

W. Edwards Deming

What are some of the problems associated with performance reviews?

- They reward those who keep the system's bureaucratic wheels well-greased. People working to improve the system are often overlooked or punished during reviews.

- They introduce competition between people who should be cooperating to produce better quality work that benefits the company. Competition between workers often breeds a "zero-sum" mentality. Why should I help you if I must compete with you for management's favor? If I stop my work to help you with yours, I must fall behind to allow you to move forward. In effect, your gain comes at my loss. Is this the philosophy we want in our workers? We think not.

- There's substantial subjectivity in performance reviews. It comes from fallible human beings with biases, emotions, and variability in their assessments. This subjectivity means that a reviewer might rate workers differently on any given day, even if they're doing the same quality of work. Worse still, studies show that human judgment varies by the day of the week, the weather, whether a favored sports team won or lost the night before, traffic jams during the morning commute, an argument with a spouse, or a host of other items irrelevant to the worker's performance [1]. It doesn't seem fair that a worker's status should be subjected to such random bias.

- We've occasionally heard management telling reviewers not to rate people too high, even if they're doing outstanding work. The rationale is that we want to leave room for them to "improve next year." We must ask ourselves if it benefits the company to downgrade someone's performance because the system can't reward excellent work year after year.

- Due to the normal statistical variability of any system, there will always be someone at the bottom. Suppose we get rid of this person. Have we then "eliminated the problem?" No, because the iron law of variability dictates that someone else must take their place. We don't believe that workers should be punished for the statistical variability of a system over which they have no control.

In our opinion, performance reviews are popular because they make it easier for managers to rate everyone and adjust staff and pay levels accordingly. Management is thereby absolved from investigating how it should work to improve the system. We believe that reviews unwittingly transfer responsibility for the system's performance from the managers, where it belongs, to their employees, who can't change the system.

Without performance reviews, managers often wonder, "How do I know who's doing a good job and who isn't?" While it's well-intentioned, we aren't sure this is the right question. Nor do we think work quality can reliably be determined via a merit system. In our view, a better question would be, "Are we providing an environment where everyone has the opportunity to reach their maximum potential?"

We believe managers should examine their work environments, creating an environment where everyone can excel in their work and lives. But this is a topic far beyond the scope of this book. What we can say is that most organizations would benefit from deep introspection in this area.

In summary, we believe performance reviews for Software Teaming groups aren't effective. Instead, we prefer to use the time and money that would otherwise have been spent on them—often a substantial sum—to maximize each worker's potential.

References

1. Kahneman, Daniel. Noise: A Flaw in Human Judgment. Little, Brown Spark. 2021.

2   Do We Recommend Software Teaming?

Illustration © 2013 - Andrea Zuill

Everyone Wants to Know: Do You Recommend Software Teaming?

Do we recommend Software Teaming for your organization? Do we recommend that your organization avoid it? The answer to both questions is: we don't know.

So how is it that we've written an entire book and can't definitively recommend anything? The simple answer is that we're cautious about recommending anything because every organization and individual is different. So many variables distinguish everyone's needs that each should be considered unique. That means that we can't make blanket recommendations that fit everyone.

What we can say is that we've been doing Software Teaming for quite a few years and think it's been working great for us. We've also seen many others adopt it, which seems to work well for them. If you're considering it, we hope this book has helped you move toward a decision.

If there's a recommendation we feel comfortable making, it's this: perhaps Software Teaming is worth considering to see if it might work for you or your organization.

To Whose Advantage?

Business environments change constantly and swiftly. It also seems that the pace of that change is accelerating. Business history is filled with stories of organizations that failed to adapt to change and suffered as a result. It's also filled with stories of those that adapted to changes in the wrong way and suffered. Where does Software Teaming fit in this view?

From a simplistic perspective, Software Teaming belongs to one of two categories:

- Software Teaming is an idea that will help businesses build software more effectively.
- Software Teaming is a costly way to build software and is best avoided.

Depending on your categorization of Software Teaming, perhaps there's a question to consider:

"If my competitors adopt Software Teaming and I don't, is that to my advantage or theirs?"

The answer to this will be based on your assessment of the viability of Software Teaming. We can't make that assessment for anyone because each organization must decide independently.

It's Not a Panacea

It's important to note that Software Teaming isn't a panacea for curing organizational ills. Software Teaming likely won't be effective if the work environment is dysfunctional or adheres to rigid, top-down decisions. Nor will it work in an environment where experimentation failures are met with punishment instead of evolutionary adaptations.

Further, Software Teaming requires a courteous and open environment where different ideas can be freely exchanged and discussed. It also works better with a disciplined development team that adheres to Agile practices like Test Driven Development, frequent inspect-and-adapt cycles, and continuous delivery. Simply put, if the work environment doesn't support Software Teaming, then it's doubtful you'll discover its benefits.

If You Decide to Try It

In the spirit of discovery, consider experimenting with Software Teaming on a small scale. We feel it's essential to move gently into something that would be such a drastic change for most teams.

- Start small
- Begin with short-term learning exercises like Code Katas
- Make participation voluntary
- Hold frequent retrospectives

For more detail, we suggest a review of Sections One and Two and the Quick Start Guide chapter. They provide the information that helps you move forward with Software Teaming.

Once you start, we suggest that you inspect and adapt continuously. If you find success, expand your experiment and see if it continues to provide benefits. If you're unable to determine this, then re-examine your approach. Can you do something differently, or will Software Teaming not work for your business? Either way, please share your results with the software community so everyone can learn.

Appendix 1 – Manifesto for Software Development

We are uncovering better ways of developing software by doing it and helping others do it. Through this work we have come to value:

Individuals and interactions over processes and tools

Working software over comprehensive documentation

Customer collaboration over contract negotiation

Responding to change over following a plan

That is, while there is value in the items on the right, we value the items on the left more.

Kent Beck, Mike Beedle, Arie van Bennekum, Alistair Cockburn, Ward Cunningham, Martin Fowler, James Grenning, Jim Highsmith, Andrew Hunt, Ron Jeffries, Jon Kern, Brian Marick, Robert C. Martin, Steve Mellor, Ken Schwaber, Jeff Sutherland, Dave Thomas

Appendix 2 – Twelve Principles of Agile Software

We follow these principles:

Our highest priority is to satisfy the customer through early and continuous delivery of valuable software.

Welcome changing requirements, even late in development.

Agile processes harness change for the customer's competitive advantage.

Deliver working software frequently, from a couple of weeks to a couple of months, with a preference to the shorter timescale.

Business people and developers must work together daily throughout the project.

Build projects around motivated individuals. Give them the environment and support they need, and trust them to get the job done.

The most efficient and effective method of conveying information to and within a development team is face-to-face conversation.

Working software is the primary measure of progress.

Agile processes promote sustainable development. The sponsors, developers, and users should be able to maintain a constant pace indefinitely.

Continuous attention to technical excellence and good design enhances agility.

Simplicity–the art of maximizing the amount of work not done–is essential.

The best architectures, requirements, and designs emerge from self-organizing teams.

At regular intervals, the team reflects on how to become more effective, then tunes and adjusts its behavior accordingly.

from http://agilemanifesto.org/principles.html

Appendix 3 – Woody's Agile Maxims

1. **It is in the doing of the work that we discover the work that we must do. Doing exposes reality.**
    a. I live this daily. Thinking about stuff is obviously worthwhile – I don't discount that. But doing is way more important.
2. **"Responding to Change" is impossible unless the code is easy to change, easy to maintain, easy to fix, easy to enhance, easy to read, and easy to discard.**
    a. The "easy qualities" – I learned them from the greatest programmer I have ever worked with: Fred Zuill, my little brother. Back in the 90's, he used to do a talk on the Qualities of Software that was pithy, meaningful, and wickedly sardonic. If you ever get a chance to hear him speak, do it. If you see him please remind him he owes me $18.
3. **Question Everything – put special focus on our deepest-held beliefs. What we trust most hides our biggest problems.**
    a. I'm pretty good at getting comfortable in my ways. Gotta work at keeping that from blocking improvement. When I really believe something, I'm likely to be fooling myself. Let's keep things uncomfortably wonky.
4. **"Working Software" is software that users are actually using. Until it's in use it is truly useless.**
    a. This is my understanding of how "Working Software" should be thought of (as in the Agile Value of "Working Software over Comprehensive Documentation").
    b. Let's not fool ourselves: "Potentially Deliverable" is a lot like "The check is in the mail."

5. **Stress at work diminishes value. Crunch-time is a symptom of harmful and counter-productive attitudes.**

    a. Nuff said? I hope so.

6. **We are the innovators of our process. Learn what works for others, prove it for ourselves, and innovate beyond.**

    a. Just a suggestion: Don't wait until you are an "expert" to innovate. Just like Jello, there is always room for innovation. (You remember those ads for Jello, don't you? Dang, you young people really missed out on the best days of television. You remember television, don't you? Dang... I'm getting old, so it seems)

7. **The object isn't to make great software. It's to be in that wonderful state which makes great software inevitable – Robert Henri, paraphrased.**

    a. This is a paraphrase of the well-known quote from Robert Henri. Just replace "great software" with the word "art" and you get the original (and much more meaningful) quote. I replay this one over and over in my head all the time. Wish I was the one who had said it! I was introduced to this quote many years ago by Donald Faast, an amazing show-card writer and sign man. I think he is in Colorado now. If you see him, just say thanks for me if you would.

8. **The more we work at the work we do, the less capable we become – Repenning/Sterman – Make time for improving capability.**

    a. Dang. If you haven't already read the paper "Nobody Ever Gets Credit for Fixing Problems that Never Happened: Creating and Sustaining Process Improvement" by Repenning and Sterman then please click on it and read that now: http://bit.ly/Qd3NmR – It's a pdf file.

9. **I reserve the right to add, remove, change, improve.**

Appendix 4 – Kevin's Official Software Teaming Certificate

There seems to be a certificate for many forms of software methodology. While it's probably a valuable undertaking for those who offer the certificates, I have reservations about their value to the recipients.

To me, certification may help with understanding the basics, but beyond that, it resembles taking a shortcut to becoming more Agile as both individuals and organizations. It's akin to paying someone to do our homework. Perhaps we'll get a short-term advantage, but it doesn't benefit us long term. It sets us up for simplistic thinking like "Three Easy Steps to Quickly Being Agile" or "Do These Three Simple Things to be Agile."

In my view, Agility isn't something distillable into a few simple steps or a certificate. It's an intellectual exercise that requires changing how we think. To believe otherwise seems like thinking that something difficult is achievable with minimal effort.

If there's anything this book has tried to indicate, however insufficiently, it's that Software Teaming is not the end goal. The end goal is to be intellectually curious, open to serendipity, and focused on creating a work environment where good things can emerge. In short, a learning environment. It's precisely this kind of environment that led to the discovery of Software Teaming. And in such environments, I'm confident that something even better will soon emerge.

Why would we want to endanger that for the rigidity of a Software Teaming certificate? Why should we risk becoming dogmatic and inflexible simply to quell our anxiety about uncertainty? We might surrender curiosity in the quest for certainty, which seems like a poor trade.

But given the industry-wide desire for certifications, it would be remiss of us if we failed to offer one. So, here goes:

> *If you read this book, then we hereby anoint you as a Certified Software Teamer. Alternatively, you are also a Certified Software Teamer if you spin around three times and throw salt over your shoulder while chanting, "I'm certified!" It helps if you burn some incense.*

So there.

You can print this out and affix it to your wall. If you read this appendix and agree with anything it says, you might also consider yourself certifiable, which may not be such a bad thing. Perhaps that's worth affixing to your wall as well.